I0045921

Sun Tzu's
THE
ART
OF
WAR

Plus

The
Art
of
Career
Building

Strategy for your Work Life

by
Gary
Gagliardi

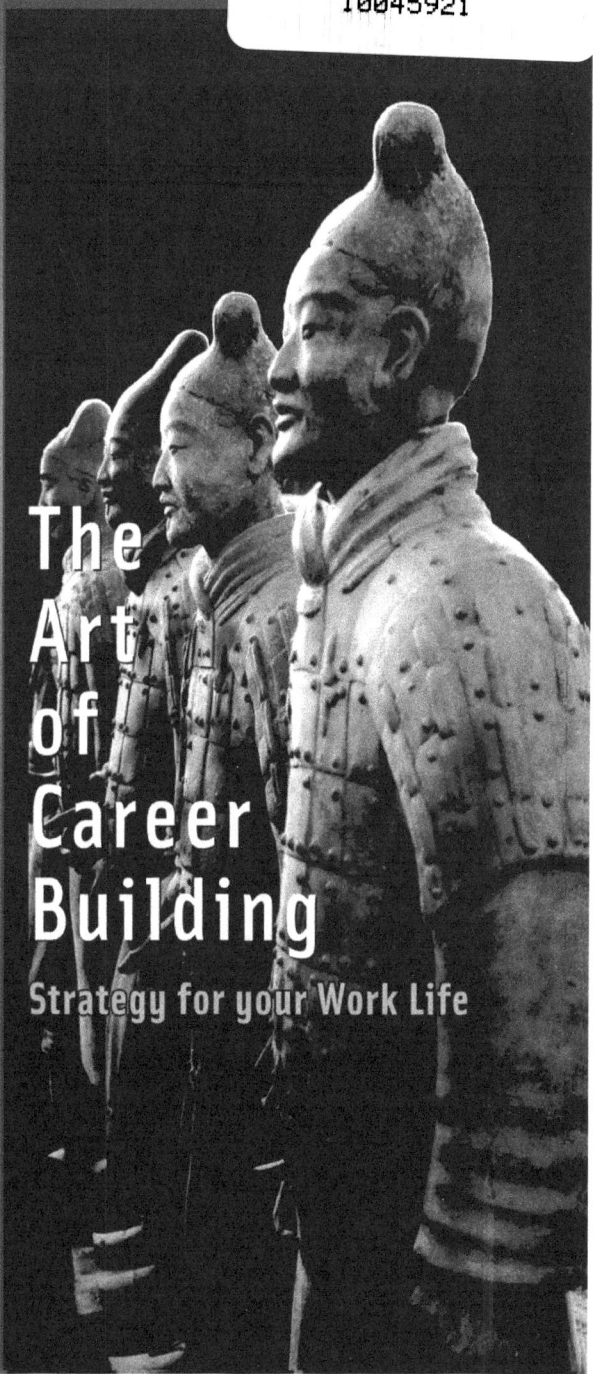

Award Recognition for *Art of War* Strategy Books
by Gary Gagliardi

The Golden Key to Strategy

Psychology/Self-Help
Ben Franklin
Book Award
2006 - Winner

Strategy Against Terror

Philosophy
Foreword Magazine
Book of the Year
2005 - Finalist

Making Money by Speaking:
The Spokesperson Strategy

Career
Foreword Magazine
Book of the Year
2007 - Finalist

Strategy for Sales Managers

Business
Independent Publishers
Book Award
2006 - Semi-Finalist

The Warrior Class:
306 Lessons in Strategy

Self-Help
Foreword Magazine
Book of the Year
2005 - Finalist

The Art of War Plus
The Art of Marketing

Business
Ben Franklin
Book Award
2004 - Finalist

The Ancient Bing-fa:
Martial Arts Strategy

Sports
Foreword Magazine
Book of the Year
2007 - Finalist

The Art of War
Plus Its Amazing Secrets

Multicultural Nonfiction
Independent Publishers
Book Award
2005 - Finalist

The Warrior's Apprentice

Youth Nonfiction
Independent Publishers
Book Award
2006 - Semi-Finalist

This book contains the complete text of the only award-winning English translation of Sun Tzu *The Art of War*.

It adapts that translation line-by-line for using Sun Tzu's methods in career competition.

The Art of War Plus
The Ancient Chinese Revealed

Multicultural Nonfiction
Independent Publishers
Book Award
2003 - Winner

Sun Tzu's

THE
ART
OF
WAR

Plus

The Art of Career Building

by Gary Gagliardi

Science of Strategy Institute
Clearbridge Publishing

Published by the Science of Strategy Institute, Clearbridge Publishing

THIRD EDITION
ISBN 978-1-929194-89-6 (13-digit) 1-929194-89-7 (10-digit)

Previously published in paperback as ISBN 1-929194-13-7 and hardcover as ISBN 1-929194-24-2
Library of Congress Catalog Card Number: 2002090338

Copyright 1999, 2000, 2001, 2003, 2007, 2011, 2013, 2014 Gary Gagliardi
All rights reserved. No part of this book may be reproduced or transmitted in any part or by any means, electronic or mechanical, including photocopying, recording, or by any information storage and retrieval system, without the written permission of the Publisher, except where
permitted by law.

Science of Strategy Institute/Clearbridge Publishing
PO Box 33772, Seattle, WA 98133
Phone: (206)542-8947 Fax: (206)546-9756
beckyw@suntzus.com
garyg@scienceofstrategy.org

Clearbridge Publishing's books may be purchased for organizations, for promotional use, or for special sales at a discount.

Manufactured in the United States of America.
Interior and cover graphic design by Dana and Jeff Wincapaw.
Original Chinese calligraphy by Tsai Yung, Green Dragon Arts, www.greendragonarts.com.

Contents

The Art of War Plus
The Art of Career Building

Foreword

A Winning Career

How does *The Art of War* apply to finding the right job, getting promoted, and the other aspects of career building? This book is about much more than warfare. The English title that focuses on war is something of a mistranslation. The Chinese title of Sun Tzu's work is:

兵bing-法fa

Though we translate this as *The Art of War*, a more accurate translation would be a single word: strategy. The English word "strategy" comes from the ancient Greek term for "thinking like a general." *Bing-fa*, meaning literally "military skill," deals with strategic planning and analysis. The fact that the book is about strategy, not war, explains why its methods apply so well to planning career moves and any other activity that requires foresight and analysis.

Sun Tzu's *Bing-Fa* offers a specific strategy for success. We call this strategy "winning without conflict." Sun Tzu's strategy consists of more than two hundred general principles. Each principle can be applied to any competitive arena in a systematic way. We call these principles *Sun Tzu's Warrior's Playbook*.

This playbook espouses using your unique position in the competitive environment to discover opportunities while turning your opponents' apparent strengths against them. This view suggests another legitimate translation of the term *bing-fa*: martial art. Sun Tzu's *Bing-Fa* is the philosophical precursor to all other martial arts. His concept of winning without conflict is the strategic equivalent of jujitsu.

Career Decision Making

Today, most readers of *The Art of War* are businesspeople looking for guidance in making better decisions. *The Art of War* offers a distinct, nonintuitive system for decision-making. It solidifies your vague idea of a strategy into a clear, well-defined set of principles. *Bing-fa* teaches that only a few key factors influence the outcome of your efforts. Success goes not to the strongest or most aggressive but to those who best understand their situation and what their alternatives really are. When you have mastered Sun Tzu's system of *bing-fa*, you will be able to almost instantly analyze competitive situations, spot opportunities, and make the appropriate decisions.

In our adaptation for career building, the basics of *bing-fa* are tailored to help you in your finding the right jobs, winning those jobs, and then getting promoted. In creating a successful career, you have to face a wide variety of issues, and we address a broad spectrum of them in this work. From Sun Tzu, we can learn how to discover the best companies for which to work, how to work within those companies for advancement, why and when to change positions in order to get ahead, and all the related issues of gaining success in your career.

As in all our *Art of War Plus* books, we present our career version side by side with our complete translation of the original text of *The Art of War*. We suggest that in reading this work, you read both texts and not just our career adaptation. Though phrased in military terms, the original text is broader in application than the issues that we address in our version for career building.

Sun Tzu's principles are simple and direct. The underlying concepts that these principles are built on, however, are rich and complex. Sun Tzu wrote precisely and succinctly, offering his ideas in a very compact format. Think of Euclid's *Geometry*. Both Euclid and Sun Tzu offer a set of basic concepts that build upon one another. Sun Tzu's principles, like Euclid's, have a wide variety of specific applications. Even within the general area of career building, they can be used in many different ways.

Why should Sun Tzu's philosophy on warfare apply so well to the problems of creating a rewarding career? It works because all competition arises from the same factors. Sun Tzu wrote about human nature, the issues of confrontation, and what matters in a contest of wills. The nature of competition has not changed in the last two thousand years and will not over the next two thousand. The only differences between competition in the job market and military warfare are the types of tools used and the nature of the battleground.

Sun Tzu realized that competition is, by its nature, a chaotic system. He used the term "chaos" in a surprisingly modern, scientific sense. He did not mean that competitive systems did not develop in an orderly way. He meant that they are complex, self-organizing systems from which patterns naturally emerge, but that we cannot predict or control specific events. Those who wish to understand the true nature of competition are well served studying modern chaos theory. If you do, you will discover that many of its principles were uncovered by Sun Tzu twenty-five hundred years ago.

Competition as Positioning

People mistakenly see war and, more generally, competition as an adversarial, destructive process, but Sun Tzu saw it as a necessary component of a productive world. He saw it as expensive but not necessarily destructive. He was familiar with the potentially destructive nature of war, but taught us how to minimize the costs of competition through logic and persuasion. He taught methods that avoid the most costly forms of conflict and yet allow us to win new positions and power.

Sun Tzu teaches that competition is simply a comparison. Competition is unavoidable because everyone is constantly comparing everything. People must compare in order to make choices. People's choices about who to hire, who to promote, and who to pay are all based on comparisons. Your choices about which skills to develop, what industries to enter, and which positions to pursue are all based on comparisons. Understanding these comparisons and how they are really made is the basis of all career positioning.

The true opposite of competition is the absence of choice. If we had no choices, we would have nothing to compare and competition wouldn't exist. Job markets wouldn't exist without a choice among different people and job positions. We must understand how employment comparisons affect both our choices about which jobs to apply for and employer's evaluations of our work.

In developing our version for careers, we were as consistent as possible in translation from the military arena to the business world. We simply define career building as a battle for better positions within the job market. A "battle" is, in Sun Tzu's system, any point at which a decisive comparison is made. The military generals addressed by Sun Tzu become today's job and promotion seekers. The nation for whom the army fights becomes the organization for which you work. The contested terrain translates into the job position or project responsibility that you desire.

What makes this interpretation so natural was Sun Tzu's economic view of warfare. Competitive comparison is based on a foundation of simple economics. In the second chapter of *The Art of War*, GOING TO WAR, Sun Tzu reflects on the costly nature of competition. The secret to competition, he concluded, is not just winning battles; it is winning in a way that enriches the nation. The secret is not victory alone: it is in making victory profitable.

This economic view maps extremely well onto any serious approach to job seeking. Our goal in career building is not just to win a job, a promotion, or even more pay; rather, it is doing so in a way that supports our success in the long term. Anyone can find a job or get a promotion. The real challenge is leveraging each step forward so that it creates even greater opportunities in the future. The choice of the wrong high-paying job can lead, surprisingly enough, to long-term unemployment.

Though *bing-fa* shows you how to find success in competitive situations, Sun Tzu's recipe for success is to avoid unnecessary conflict. Competition is comparison, not conflict. He sees conflict as inherently costly. He teaches you how to handle direct, hostile confrontations when they cannot be avoided, but his basic approach is to defuse these situations before they occur. His method is psychological: you must convince potential opponents to give you what you want without a fight. Again, this closely matches the goals in workplace. You must convince potential opponents and rivals that your success also promotes their own success. Sun Tzu taught the art of persuasion as an alternative to destructive confrontations in competitive situations.

In building your career, your purpose shouldn't be just to get a good job, but to find a position that creates more opportunities for you in the job market. Your only resource is your time. Your time is limited. You must use your limited time as efficiently as possible to create the most successful career possible. The last thing that you can afford is to be trapped a dead-end job in a stagnant company working only for a paycheck.

When we adapt Sun Tzu's methods of warfare to career building, the lessons that emerge from Sun Tzu are intriguing. First, Sun Tzu teaches that winning a job is not enough. The goal is to win easily with minimal risk. The first step in finding a better job is doing well in our existing job. We never want to be in a position of looking for a new job because we are out of work. People who are out of work never get the best jobs unless they are in the process of creating their own company. We only want to fight for a position in situations where we are certain to win, but we also want to be certain that winning is well worth the cost. In most of the career-building adaptation, we do not discriminate between changing jobs within a company and finding a job in a different company. In Sun Tzu's system, both are competitive moves that must be carefully evaluated before they are undertaken.

Sun Tzu is specific about what to do in certain situations. He wants us to pay close attention to the details of our work situation. He enumerates different job conditions, different types of opponents, different potential decision-making mistakes, different competitive signals, and so on. Although Sun Tzu wrote 2,500 years ago about warfare, when translated to career building, his detailed lists are still surprisingly complete. His advice is useful to anyone planning their career.

Sun Tzu offers a "cooperative" view of competition. In his mind's eye, we cannot win through our own actions. We do not create our next job opportunity. We can perform in our existing job very well, but we discover new opportunities only when others create them. The secret is recognizing a good opportunity when it presents itself. A pay raise alone is not an opportunity. We must always be looking for broader, more important positions where we can solve someone's problem.

Finally, Sun Tzu's view of competition is knowledge-intensive. Sun Tzu sees victory going to the person who is the most knowledgeable. He even recognizes creativity as a special type of knowledge. In Sun Tzu, there is no substitute for good information. We are beginning to realize that people in the economy are paid for their knowledge, but knowledge in Sun Tzu's system is more than knowing what we need to do our job at the moment. It means learning our industry from top to bottom.

As you read this book, notice how closely *The Art of Career Building* follows Sun Tzu's original ideas in *The Art of War*. While *The Art of Career Building* applies Sun Tzu's ideas in ways that he would never have foreseen, it does so respecting the integrity of his thinking. We follow his advice and admonitions as closely as possible, line by line.

Your Changing Situation

The universal utility of Sun Tzu's principles means that you can apply them in different ways in different situations. With more study, you will develop more insight into Sun Tzu's methods and your own situation.

As your situation changes, different parts of the book will become more important. In general, the book is organized so that the broadest and longest-term issues, such as strategic analysis, are addressed in the initial chapters. Later chapters tend to focus on the special challenges encountered under specific conditions.

Later chapters tend to focus on the special challenges encountered under specific conditions of a changing career path. Do not expect to appreciate all of Sun Tzu's principles in one reading. Time spent studying Sun Tzu's system of strategility is always time well invested.

Reading this book is simply the first step in mastering the warrior's world of competitive philosophy. As I have said, Sun Tzu's strategic system is sophisticated and deep. Much of its sophistication is not readily apparent simply from reading the text. The Science of Strategy Institute has spent more than a decade detailing the use of Sun Tzu's principles in today's increasingly competitive world. This career adaptation helps you start using Sun Tzu's ideas, but if you are interested in mastering this powerful competitive strategy in business generally and advancing your career specifically, it only scratches the surface of what is hidden in the work.

If you want to continue your study of Sun Tzu's principles, please visit SunTzus.com. Every day on that site, we explain one of Sun Tzu's general principles in detail. Those who become paid members of the Institute get on-line access to our complete *Sun Tzu's Art of War Playbook*, which explains hundreds of Sun Tzu's principles in terms of simple step-by-step rules. The

Institute also offers a number of audio books, seminars, and—most importantly —on-line training courses to make Sun Tzu's methods instinctive.

When we started codifying Sun Tzu's strategic rules, we didn't realize how big the task was. In the end, the work encompassed over two hundred and thirty articles. Each article explains one strategic principle and its relationships to interconnected principles. Developed as a framework for a complete course of strategic studies, these articles break down each general principle into a series of steps or components that are illustrated by examples from modern competition. These articles have been organized into nine areas of strategic skill. These articles now are also available in nine volumes, each focusing on a single strategic skill area, both as ebooks and as printed books.

Why is this work on developing Sun Tzu's ideas into rules necessary? As you will see in reading this work, Sun Tzu's *The Art of War* is not a "training book" in the modern Western sense. It is a list of formulas written the context of the scientific philosophy of the era. Adapting these ideas into the terms of modern marketing is a start, but understanding all these concepts is nearly impossible for modern readers without examples or exercises. Like Euclid's Geometry, simply reading the work gives us few useful tools. Our development of the *Playbook* and our training exercises was necessary to help people practice in these methods in their everyday life.

✦ ✦ ✦

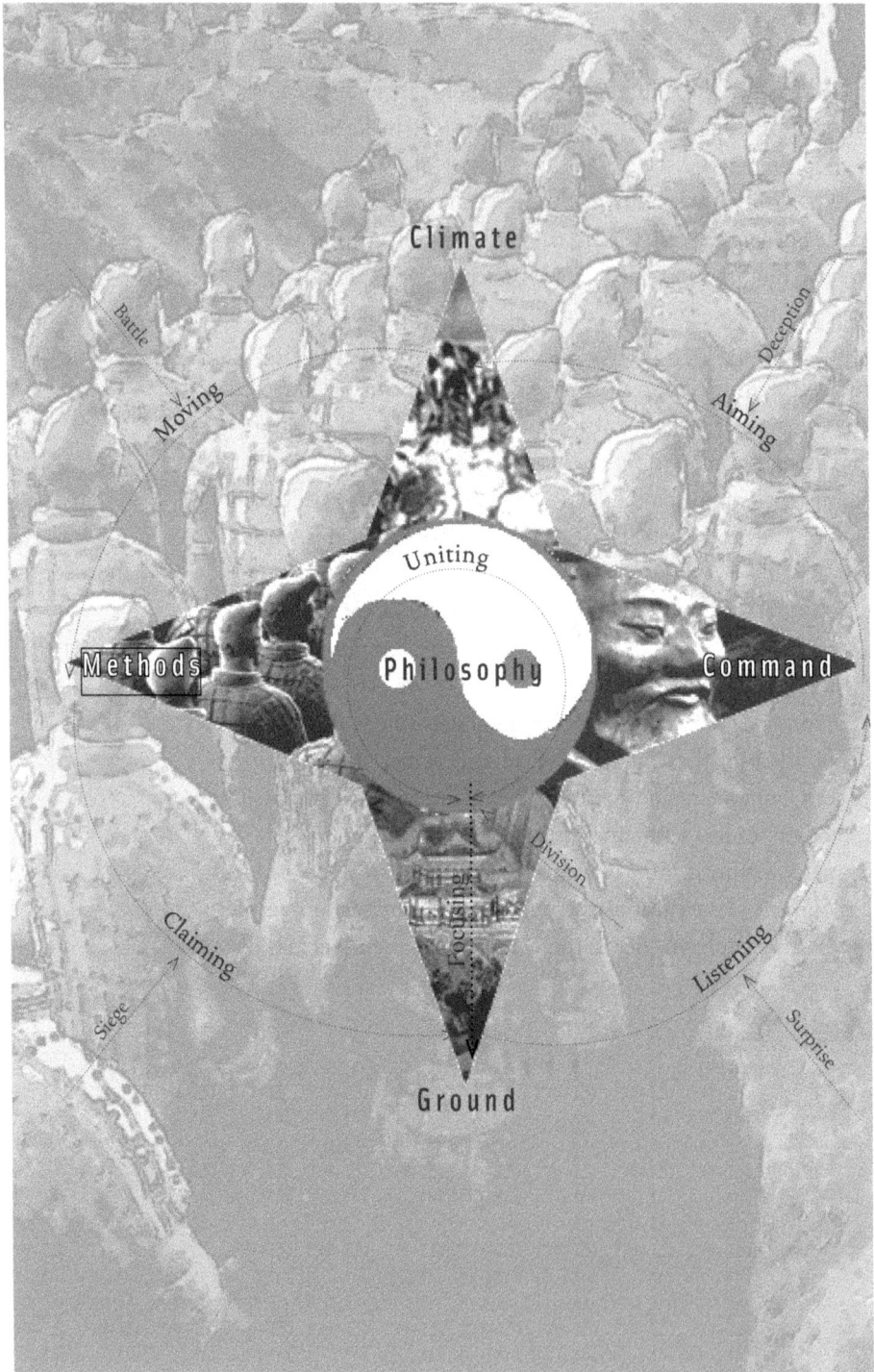

Climate

Battle

Moving

Deception

Aiming

Uniting

Methods

Philosophy

Command

Claiming

Division

Siege

Focusing

Listening

Surprise

Ground

Introduction:

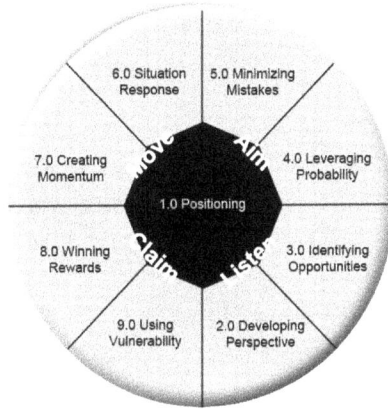

6.0 Situation Response 5.0 Minimizing Mistakes
7.0 Creating Momentum 4.0 Leveraging Probability
1.0 Positioning
8.0 Winning Rewards 3.0 Identifying Opportunities
9.0 Using Vulnerability 2.0 Developing Perspective

Sun Tzu's Basic Concepts

This book teaches the use of classical strategy to achieve success in your career. To put you on the path of continually advancing career, let us clarify the elements of Sun Tzu's strategic system. If you are new to Sun Tzu's strategic principles, you will find *The Art of War* and our career adaptation, *The Art of Career Building*, much easier to understand if you first familiarize yourself with a few basic concepts, metaphors, and analogies. As with all traditional Chinese science, this system is based on five elements and the nine skills. This introduction gives you an overview of these elements of his strategic system.

As defined by Sun Tzu, strategy is not a system of planning. Planning, in the sense of prioritizing a list of activities, works in controlled environments where you can know how others will respond to your decisions. Strategy works in competitive environments where your decisions collide with the decisions of others, creating conditions that no one planned. In competitive environments, your success depends on predicting how others will respond.

Sun Tzu taught that in these competitive environments, success is not a matter of winning fights with other people. Instead success depends on building and advancing strategic positions. The idea is to create positions that others cannot attack and that ideally they want to join. Sun Tzu teaches that a general who fights a hundred battles and wins a hundred battles is not a good general. A good general is one who finds a way to win without fighting a single battle. Strategy teaches that you win by building the right positions and advancing those positions while avoiding conflict.

The Five Elements

Sun Tzu's strategic tool kit is based on the *five element system* introduced in the first section of his first chapter. These five elements—philosophy, heaven, ground, the leader, and methods—define a strategic position and provide the backbone of strategic analysis. All the other components of his system—deception, unity, knowledge, and so on—have very specific and logical relationships to these five elements. The depth and sophistication of the system require some explanation.

Sun Tzu taught that every competitive situation depends upon the unique position of a given competitor within the larger competitive environment. This position is what is compared to other positions. Understanding positions is the first skill that his strategic system teaches.

Sun Tzu's strategy is focused on building up or advancing your position in such a way that opponents cannot attack you and ideally others want to join you. In choosing between your and a competitor, the employer decides based upon your relative positions within this larger competitive environment. All the other skills of his toolkit for advancing positions—developing perspective, identifying opportunities, and so on (see the first diagram in this introduction)—develop better positions from these elements.

The focus on the competitive environment was a unique feature of Sun Tzu's work, at least until Darwin. As with so many of Sun Tzu's basic concepts, he describes the environment as two opposite and yet complementary halves, *heaven (climate)* and *ground (earth)*. Heaven and ground are the arenas of time and place within which you compete for your employer' dollars.

Heaven represents the uncontrollable passage of time, but more accurately it describes change. It is often translated as "climate" or "weather" in the text. It is best to think of heaven as trends that change over time. The cycle of the seasons is the most obvious trend in the natural environment, but every organization has its own business cycle and job climate. People's attitudes and emotions are also an important part of Sun Tzu's concept of climate. Changes in the general economy, industry trends, hiring cycles, government regulation, and the hiring process all affect your career. Each change is an opportunity to change people's minds about your value. These business cycles cannot be controlled but they can be recognized and, to some degree, predicted.

Ground is the economic foundation on which your strategic position is based. It is both where you compete and what you compete for. As an employee, you can think of the ground as your job markets, your competitors, and your potential employers. Unlike heaven, which is largely beyond your control, the most important aspect of the ground is that you choose where you compete. So the battle ground results only from your choices and actions. You choose your employer. You choose what to say about your abilities and goals. Choosing positions, moving to them, and utilizing them are the basis of Sun Tzu's strategic methods.

The first two components of your strategic position define the external time and place of your strategic position.

You and your job are positioned within a *heaven* of changing job market trends. All job positions represent a prediction about what is important for the future. Your employers are making decisions today about what will be important in the future. You are making decisions about the future. All the emotions involved in the employment cycle are based upon the fears and uncertainties about what the future will bring.

Your strategic position is grounded on the world (*earth*) of real job positions. Your employers are your base of financial support. You battle with competitors for the limited number of positions and with fellow employees for a limited amount your employer can afford to spend on wages. Correctly analyzing this ground and picking the right employers is the basis of your success.

Within the larger competitive environment, the unique characteristics of both you and your skills are also part of your strategic position. Sun Tzu breaks the important characteristics of a competitor into two opposite and complementary components: the *leader* and *methods*.

A *leader* is a person who makes the decisions in a contest. Employees are leaders because they must make job choices. All employer are also leaders, that is, decision-makers beause they choose who to hire ad what to pay. Leadership is the realm of individual character. A leader masters the strategy so that he or she can make the right decisions quickly.

Methods are the skills of a person, an organization, and an industry. Success depends upon working with other people. Methods are the realm where you interact with other people. Employers and employees make decisions as individuals, but you must work with fellow employers, managers, and your organization's suppliers. You must also connect to your organization's customers and ultimately, provide them value. The job of career building is to connect your personal skills to the skills of others to create the most value in the job market.

Binding and underlying your strategic position is its *philosophy*. *Philosophy* is the unique values that provide the core of a strategic position. In a organization, we call this a company mission or purpose. Your personal philosophy is what you work for. Money is part of this, but so are a lot of other things: job satisfaction, stability, appreciation and so on.

In Sun Tzu's system, philosophy is a shared goal. You must satisfy your goals by satisfying your organization's goals. A shared philosophy provides organzations with unity and focus. The closer your and your organization's goals and values align, the stronger your connection.

Listen Aim Move Claim

Once you see your strategic position clearly in terms of these five factors, you advance your position. The balance of the book addresses specific methods a person can use for advancing a job position. However, all this information can be boiled down into four simple steps. Sun Tzu's terms for these four processes are *knowing, foreseeing, moving,* and *positioning*. More generally, we describe these steps are *listening for knowledge, aiming at opportunities, moving to openings,* and *claiming a position*. Every advance requires all four steps. If you miss a step, the process is more likely to create problems than to solve them.

Knowledge comes from understanding your ground, which requires *listening. Aim* means seeing how changing trends create an *opportunity* to advance. *Moving* means the ability to change methods to take advantage of an *opening. Claiming* means reaping the rewards from a new ground *position*.

These four steps can be further broken down into a list of eight skills. Remember, Sun Tzu's first skill is understanding positions. Listening requires Sun Tzu's second key strategic skill of an outside developing perspective on your position and his third strategic skill of using change for identifying opportunities. Aiming requires Sun Tzu's fourth and fifth skills, leveraging probability and minimizing mistakes. Moving requires his six and seventh skills of situation response and creating momentum. Claiming requires his eighth and ninth skills of winning rewards and understanding vulnerabilities. All of these skills are covered in detail in our *Sun Tzu's Playbook*, referenced at the end of each chapter.

Positioning and these four steps for advancing a position provides the basis for the nine skills taught in the nine volumes of *Sun Tzu's Playbook*. Positioning is the concept taught in the first volume. Listening is covered in the second and third volumes: 2. Developing Perspective, and 3. Identifying Opportunities. Aiming is the focus of the fourth and fifth volumes: 4. Leveraging Probability, and 5. Minimizing Mistakes. Moving requires the skills taught in the sixth and seventh voluments: 6. Responding To Situations and 7. Creating Momentum. Claiming is the basis of the last two volumes: 8. Winning Rewards, and 9. Defending Vulnerabilities.

Each of these four steps and eight skills leads naturally to the next in an endless cycle of advances. In advancing your career, they form a spiral, working from the your first low-skilled job to advancement to more skilled and more rewarding work. Each promotion or new job improves your position for the next cycle of advance. The more you learn about your ground, the more you need to identify new opportunities. Aiming at a new opportunity necessitates moving to develop new skills or methds. Moving must give you a new job position or title that you can claim. Claiming new ground creates new opportunities to listen and learn. Even if your attempted advance fails to yield profitable new ground, it cannot fail to generate new knowledge, which is the basis of your next cycle and your inevitable success in your career.

Consciously or unconsciously, you go through this cycle every time you advance your position. When a decision is unsuccessful, it is simply because one of these four steps was not properly executed.

The Art of War is a complete guide to executing these four steps in a wide variety of situations. However, much of it is written in a kind of code. These four steps are usually referenced in terms metaphors. Listening for knowledge is referenced as sound.

Thunder, music, and drums are all metaphors for listening. Aim is described as vision. Colors, lightning, and so on are all metaphors for foresight. Moving is marching. Claiming a position is variously described as gathering food, building, eating, digging in, and so on. We make all of these ideas easier to understand by adapting these metaphors into more easily understood management terms.

Just as these four steps are defined in terms of the five factors of a position, other strategic responses are defined in terms of these four steps. *Surprise* undermines knowledge. *Deception* confuses aim. *Battle*—which means meeting a challenge, not necessarily conflict— counters movement. *Siege* tries to overturn a position.

For a picture of Sun Tzu's system of five elements, four steps, and four responses, you can refer to the diagram that precedes this introduction.

✦ ✦ ✦

Heaven
Philosophy
Methods   Leader
Ground

Chapter 1

計

Analysis (Career Planning)

Although Sun Tzu named his first chapter 計 in Chinese, which translates to "plan" or "planning" in English, his meaning is much closer to what we would call competitive analysis. As you manage your career, you must perform this type of analysis frequently.

In the chapter's first section, Sun Tzu describes the major components that make up competitive systems.

In the next section, he describes how to directly compare your competitive situation with that of your competitors.

He stresses in the next section the need for good information for competitive analysis, especially information from outsiders.

The discussion in the following section moves from the value of information to the value of controlling information, or what Sun Tzu calls the use of deception. By "deception," he doesn't mean dishonesty—on the contrary, honesty is one of the necessary characteristics of a leader. His idea of deception would equate much more closely to consciously controlling other people's perceptions.

In the chapter's final section, Sun Tzu introduces the idea that competitive analysis is a quantitative art: a balancing of pros and cons.

All of these ideas are covered in more detail in later chapters, but here he provides an introductory overview.

Analysis

Sun Tzu said:

This is war. 1
It is the most important skill in the nation.
It is the basis of life and death.
It is the philosophy of survival or destruction.
You must know it well.

[6]Your skill comes from five factors.
Study these factors when you plan war.
You must insist on knowing your situation.

1.	Discuss philosophy.
2.	Discuss the climate.
3.	Discuss the ground.
4.	Discuss leadership.
5.	Discuss military methods.

[14]It starts with your military philosophy.
Command your people in a way that gives them a higher
shared purpose.
You can lead them to death.
You can lead them to life.
They must never fear danger or dishonesty.

Career Planning

1 This is career building.
It is the central focus of your professional life.
It is the foundation of prosperity or poverty.
It is the basis of your progress or stagnation.
You must analyze your career.

Five factors determine your professional success.
Evaluate these factors when planning your career.
You must insist on understanding your situation.

1.   Think about your professional goals.
2.   Think about the trends in the job market.
3.   Think about your career options.
4.   Think about your job skills.
5.   Think about your career-building methods.

Career building begins with your professional goals.
You must see your working life as having a higher purpose than
simply earning a paycheck.
Your decisions can lead to failure.
Your decisions can lead to success.
You must be careful and never lie to yourself.

[19] Next, you have the climate.
It can be sunny or overcast.
It can be hot or cold.
It includes the timing of the seasons.

[23] Next is the terrain.
It can be distant or near.
It can be difficult or easy.
It can be open or narrow.
It also determines your life or death.

[28] Next is the commander.
He must be smart, trustworthy, caring, brave, and strict.

[30] Finally, you have your military methods.
They include the shape of your organization.
This comes from your management philosophy.
You must master their use.

[34] All five of these factors are critical.
As a commander, you must pay attention to them.
Understanding them brings victory.
Ignoring them means defeat.

Next are the trends in the job market.
The business climate can be either good or bad.
Certain jobs grow more important with time.
The trends in the job market will change over time.

Next are your career options.
You can stay with an existing employer or change companies.
You can look for a challenge or something easy.
You can be wide open to new ideas or be very selective.
Choosing the right path determines your success or failure.

Next are your job skills.
You must be bright, trustworthy, likeable, brave, and disciplined.

Finally, you need a process for building your career.
It must include a network of business contacts.
Your methods arise naturally from your career goals.
You must become comfortable with seeking advancement.

All five of these factors are critical.
You must continuously evaluate them.
Your success depends on them.
Disregarding them leads to failure.

You must learn through planning. 2
You must question the situation.

³You must ask:
Which government has the right philosophy?
Which commander has the skill?
Which season and place has the advantage?
Which method of command works?
Which group of forces has the strength?
Which officers and men have the training?
Which rewards and punishments make sense?
This tells when you will win and when you will lose.
Some commanders perform this analysis.
If you use these commanders, you will win.
Keep them.
Some commanders ignore this analysis.
If you use these commanders, you will lose.
Get rid of them.

Plan an advantage by listening 3
Adjust to the situations.
Get assistance from the outside.
Influence events.
Then planning can find opportunities and give you control.

2 Career planning requires constant analysis.
You need to continually question your situation.

You must ask this:
Which opportunities are consistent with your goals?
Are you developing your job skills?
When and where should you look for new positions?
Which career advancement techniques work best?
Which groups have control over your professional future?
Which opportunities give you training for the future?
What risks and rewards make sense?
This analysis tells you where you can and cannot advance.
You must continually do such career analysis.
If you plan your career, you will be successful.
Keep at it.
Most people never plan their careers.
If you are one of them, you will go nowhere.
You must change.

3 Career planning forces you to listen to other people.
Knowledge of the job market makes you powerful.
Get help from people outside your company.
Know your job situation.
Planning uncovers your strengths and directs your energies.

Warfare is one thing. 4
It is a philsophy of deception.

3When you are ready, you try to appear incapacitated.
When active, you pretend inactivity.
When you are close to the enemy, you appear distant.
When far away, you pretend you are near.

7If the enemy has a strong position, entice him away from it.
If the enemy is confused, be decisive.
If the enemy is solid, prepare against him.
If the enemy is strong, avoid him.
If the enemy is angry, frustrate him.
If the enemy is weaker, make him arrogant.
If the enemy is relaxed, make him work.
If the enemy is united, break him apart.
Attack him when he is unprepared.
Leave when he least expects it.

17You will find a place where you can win.
You cannot first signal your intentions.

4 Career building means one thing:
It means controlling people's perceptions of you.

If you are unprepared, you must appear prepared.
If you are working hard, you must make it look easy.
When close to making a job change, appear willing to wait.
When no move is planned, appear ready for a change.

When a good position is available, court it.
When others are uncertain, be decisive.
When the job market becomes competitive, protect yourself.
When someone is entrenched, move around his position.
If a hiring decision is emotional, play to that emotion.
If your job rivals are weak, make them overconfident.
If a pontential employer is indifferent, make him wake up.
If a job change requires agreement, line up supporters.
Go after positions that others have overlooked.
Leave a job when others least expected it.

You can often find a position that advances your career.
Never pass it by.

Manage to avoid battle until your organization can count 5
on certain victory.
You must calculate many advantages.
Before you go to battle, your organization's analysis can
indicate that you may not win.
You can count few advantages.
Many advantages add up to victory.
Few advantages add up to defeat.
How can you know your advantages without analyzing them?
We can see where we are by means of our observations.
We can foresee our victory or defeat by planning.

5 Before going after a new job, you must know that you can win it.

You must know that you are the most qualified.

Do not waste your efforts; you must avoid jobs that you cannot win easily.

You must know when you do not have the qualifications.

Good qualifications add up to winning the position.

Poor qualifications add up to losing the position.

How can you build your qualifications without planning?

You must know how well you are doing where you are.

You can control your advancement by planning.

♦ ♦ ♦

Related Articles from *Sun Tzu's Playbook*

In this first chapter, Sun Tzu introduces the basics of positioning. We explore these ideas in more detail in our Sun Tzu's Art of War Playbook. To learn the step-by-step techniques for positioning, we recommend the Playbook articles listed below.

1.0.0 Strategic Positioning: developing relatively superior positions.

1.1.0 Position Paths: the continuity of strategic positions over time.

1.1.1 Position Dynamics: how all current positions evolve over time.

1.1.2 Defending Positions: defending current positions until new positions are established.

1.2 Subobjective Positions: the subjective and objective aspects of a position.

1.2.1 Competitive Landscapes: the arenas in which rivals jockey for position.

1.2.2 Exploiting Exploration: how competitive landscapes are searched and positions identified.

1.2.3 Position Complexity: how positions arise from interactions in complex environments.

1.3 Elemental Analysis: the relevant components of all competitive positions.

1.3.1 Competitive Comparison: competition as the comparison of positions.

1.3.2 Element Scalability: how elements of a position scale up to larger positions.

1.4 The External Environment: external conditions shaping strategic positions.

1.4.1 Climate Shift: forces of environmental change shaping temporary conditions.

1.4.2 Ground Features: the persistent resources that we can control.

1.5 Competing Agents: the key characteristics of competitors.

1.5.1 Command Leadership: individual decision-making.

1.5.2. Group Methods: systems for executing decisions.

1.6 Mission Values: the goals and values needed for motivation.

1.6.1 Shared Mission: finding goals that others can share.

1.6.2 Types of Motivations: hierarchies of motivation that define missions.

1.6.3 Shifting Priorities: how missions change according to temporary conditions.

Chapter 2

作戰

Going to War (Changing Jobs)

After introducing the key elements of competition, Sun Tzu focuses on the economic consequences of war. Sun Tzu does not define victory as simply winning battles. He specifically defines success as making victory pay. This economic focus is one of the reasons that this strategy works so well in today's business world. With regard to success in your career, this chapter addresses the economic dangers of changing to a new job.

Sun Tzu starts by discussing the debilitating cost of competition and how easily money is wasted.

The next short section describes the total cost and total reward of competition as unpredictable. Sun Tzu therefore advises minimizing spending to necessities.

Sun Tzu then covers the effect of distance on cost. He explains why organizations that are unable to control costs are doomed.

He then offers his strategy for cost control: making every competitive venture pay for itself as directly and quickly as possible. He calls this "feeding off of the enemy."

In the chapter's final section, Sun Tzu argues that the ability to control costs is the key to a stable organization and that this depends on the knowledge of the leader.

Going to War

SUN TZU SAID:

Everything depends on your use of military philosophy. 1
Moving the army requires thousands of vehicles.
These vehicles must be loaded thousands of times.
The army must carry a huge supply of arms.
You need ten thousand acres of grain.
This results in internal and external shortages.
Any army consumes resources like an invader.
It uses up glue and paint for wood.
It requires armor for its vehicles.
People complain about the waste of a vast amount of metal.
It will set you back when you attempt to raise tens of
thousands of troops.

[12]Using a huge army makes war very expensive to win.
Long delays create a dull army and sharp defeats.
Attacking enemy cities drains your forces.
Long violent campaigns that exhaust the nation's resources
are wrong.

Changing Jobs

1 Everything depends on your career goals.
Building a career requires thousands of decisions.
Building a career involves finding new positions.
You must develop a host of skills.
You must invest time and energy.
Career building takes time away from your family.
It can destroy your life if you let it.
It requires creativity and imagination.
It demands that you perform your existing job well.
People will always complain about what they are paid.
You will fall behind in your career if you take a job simply because it
pays more.

A big paycheck can make moving to the right job difficult.
Staying too long in the wrong job leads to failure.
Attacking an entrenched superior drains your energy.
A long period in a stagnant position that drains your career
momentum is wrong.

[16]Manage a dull army.
You will suffer sharp defeats.
Drain your forces.
Your money will be used up.
Your rivals will multiply as your army collapses and they will
begin against you.
It doesn't matter how smart you are.
You cannot get ahead by taking losses!

[23]You hear of people going to war too quickly.
Still, you won't see a skilled war that lasts a long time.

[25]You can fight a war for a long time or you can make your
nation strong.
You can't do both.

Make no assumptions about all the dangers in using **2**
military force.
Then you won't make assumptions about the benefits of
using arms either.

[3]You want to make good use of war.
Do not raise troops repeatedly.
Do not carry too many supplies.
Choose to be useful to your nation.
Feed off the enemy.
Make your army carry only the provisions it needs.

You can get stuck in the wrong job.

Then you will find yourself doing poorly.

It drains your energy.

The paycheck that holds you is soon spent.

As your enthusiasm for the job fades, you inspire internal rivals to attack you.

It does not matter how smart you think you are.

You cannot get ahead once you have lost the initiative.

You can sometimes move between jobs too quickly.

However, the slower your progress, the more often you fail.

You can be lazy when you looking for a new position or you can be successful.

You can't have it both ways.

2 You can never completely insure against failure when you move into a new position.

Nor can you know all the opportunities that will arise from moving into a new position.

You must make good use of your existing position.

Do not repeatedly ask for raises.

Do not accumulate large debts.

Choose to be invaluable to your employer.

Get rewarded for your value to your employer.

Spend only the money you absolutely must.

The nation impoverishes itself shipping to troops that **3** are far away.

Distant transportation is costly for hundreds of families.

Buying goods with the army nearby is also expensive.

High prices also exhaust wealth.

If you exhaust your wealth, you then quickly hollow out your military.

Military forces consume a nation's wealth entirely.

War leaves households in the former heart of the nation with nothing.

[8]War destroys hundreds of families.

Out of every ten families, war leaves only seven.

War empties the government's storehouses.

Broken armies will get rid of their horses.

They will throw down their armor, helmets, and arrows.

They will lose their swords and shields.

They will leave their wagons without oxen.

War will consume sixty percent of everything you have.

Because of this, it is the intelligent commander's duty is **4** to feed off the enemy.

[2]Use a cup of the enemy's food.

It is worth twenty of your own.

Win a bushel of the enemy's feed.

It is worth twenty of your own.

3 Relocating to a new city to start working in a new position is expensive.

Traveling to interview for a new position is costly.

Staying in a crowded job market is also expensive.

Staying in a weak job market impoverishes you.

You can quickly exhaust your bank account looking for work.

Paying employment agencies can consume your financial resources entirely.

Looking for work can impoverish your entire family and leave you with nothing.

The economy is risky.

Companies go out of business.

Competition pressures everyone in the job market.

People without jobs will take any position.

They are willing to work for low pay and benefits.

They do not worry about protecting themselves.

They are worried about losing their houses and cars.

Without work, people will lose the assets they have built up.

4 Because of this, your success comes from making your employer successful.

Take a dollar of pay in shared profits.

It is worth twenty dollars in salary.

Win bonuses based on your performance.

They are worth twenty times more than guarantees.

[6]You can kill the enemy and frustrate him as well.
Take the enemy's strength from him by stealing away his
money.

[8]Fight for the enemy's supply wagons.
Capture his supplies by using overwhelming force.
Reward the first who capture them.
Then change their banners and flags.
Mix them in with your own wagons to increase your supply
line.
Keep your soldiers strong by providing for them.
This is what it means to beat the enemy while you grow
more powerful.

Make victory in war pay for itself. 5
Avoid expensive, long campaigns.
The military commander's knowledge is the key.
It determines if the civilian officials can govern.
It determines if the nation's households are peaceful or a
danger to the state.

✦ ✦ ✦

You must be productive and indispensable.

You must generate more value in the business than your pay consumes.

Fight for business for your employer.

Focus all your efforts on making your company a success.

Insist on being rewarded for your efforts.

Insist on being recognized for the business you've won.

If your company is successful, it will be able to reward and promote you.

Your job will be secure because you are needed.

This is what it means to win in competition while building your career.

5 Make your job search pay for itself.

Avoid staying in the same position for too long.

Your knowledge of your field is the key.

It determines your ability to manage your career.

It determines how valuable you are as an employee and how easily you can move up.

♦ ♦ ♦

Related Articles from *Sun Tzu's Playbook*

In his second chapter, Sun Tzu teaches basic competitive economics. We explore these ideas in more detail in our Sun Tzu's Art of War Playbook. *To learn the step-by-step techniques for economical political campaigning, we recommend the articles listed below.*

1.3.1 Competitive Comparison: competition as the comparison of positions.

1.6.1 Shared Mission: finding goals that others can share.

1.8.3 Cycle Time: speed in feedback and reaction.

1.8.4 Probabilistic Process: the role of chance in strategic processes and systems.

2.2.1 Personal Relationships: how information depends on personal relationships.

2.2.2 Mental Models: how mental models simplify decision-making.

2.3.4 Using Questions: using questions in gathering information and predicting reactions.

3.1 Strategic Economics: balancing the cost and benefits of positioning.

3.1.1 Resource Limitations: the inherent limitation of strategic resources.

3.1.2 Strategic Profitability: understanding gains and losses.

3.1.3 Conflict Cost: the costly nature of resolving competitive comparisons by conflict.

3.1.4 Openings: seeking openings to avoid costly conflict.

3.1.5 Unpredictable Value: the limitations of predicting the value of positions.

3.1.6 Time Limitations: the time limits on opportunities.

4.0 Leveraging Probability: better decisions regarding our choice of opportunities.

4.1 Future Potential: the limitations and potential of current and future positions.

4.2 Choosing Non-Action: choosing between action and non-action.

5.3 Reaction Time: the use of speed in choosing actions.

5.3.1 Speed and Quickness: the use of pace within a dynamic environment.

5.3.2 Opportunity Windows: the effect of speed upon opposition.

5.3.3 Information Freshness: choosing actions based on freshness of information.

5.4 Minimizing Action: minimizing waste, i.e., less is more.

5.4.1 Testing Value : choosing actions to test for value.

5.4.2 Successful Mistakes: learning from our mistakes.

5.5 Focused Power: size consideration in safe experimentation.

5.5.1 Force Size: limiting the size of force in an advance.

5.5.2 Distance Limitations: the use of short steps to reach distant goals.

Chapter 3

謀攻

Planning an Attack (Picking the Right Job)

The central topic of this chapter is unity and focus and their effect on the relative strength of an organization. In terms of advancing your career, the important lesson here is that you must pick the proper focus for your career-building efforts.

In the chapter's first section, Sun Tzu says that unity and focus are required at every level of an organization. The goal of unity is not to win battles, but to succeed without battle.

Sun Tzu then lists the basic forms of attack in decending order of importance. The text warns against the worst of these: laying siege to another's strong position.

In the third section, Sun Tzu suggests an incremental approach to success: fighting small, focused battles where you have the clear advantage. He explains how the relative strength of competitive forces determines your basic tactics.

The text then warns against political divisions within an organization and how these divisions weaken its competitive strength.

Sun Tzu then details the five areas of knowledge that determine your ability to unite and concentrate your forces.

He ends with a warning about the dangers in miscalculating the relative strength of your organization of facing competition.

Planning an Attack

SUN TZU SAID:

Everyone relies on the arts of war. 1
A united nation is strong.
A divided nation is weak.
A united army is strong.
A divided army is weak.
A united force is strong.
A divided force is weak.
United men are strong.
Divided men are weak.
A united unit is strong.
A divided unit is weak.

[12]Unity works because it enables you to win every battle you
fight.
Still, this is the foolish goal of a weak leader.
Avoid battle and make the enemy's men surrender.
This is the right goal for a superior leader.

The best policy is to attack while the enemy is still planning. 2
The next best is to disrupt alliances.
The next best is to attack the opposing army.
The worst is to attack the enemy's cities.

Picking the Right Job

1 Everyone depends on the rules of competition.
A focused organization will be successful.
An unfocused organization will fail.
A united team can accomplish anything.
A divided team accomplishes nothing.
A concentrated effort creates success.
A disconnected effort creates confusion.
Well-integrated skills make you desirable.
Disconnected skills makes you undesirable.
Clear-cut goals make you successful.
Confused goals lead to failure.

The more focused you are, the easier it will be to overcome career challenges.
But overcoming difficulty doesn't make a great career.
Avoid difficulties and stand out clearly from your rivals.
This is the right path for a successful career.

2 It's best to win a new position while it is still being planned.
The next best is to get a job through connections.
The next best is to win a promotion by beating competitors.
The worst is to go after someone else's secure position.

5This is what happens when you attack a city.
You can attempt it, but you can't finish it.
First you must make siege engines.
You need the right equipment and machinery.
It takes three months and still you cannot win.
Then you try to encircle the area.
You use three more months without making progress.
Your command still doesn't succeed and this angers you.
You then try to swarm the city.
This kills a third of your officers and men.
Your are still unable to draw the enemy out of the city.
This attack is a disaster.

Make good use of war. 3
Make the enemy's troops surrender.
You can do this fighting only minor battles.
You can draw their men out of their cities.
You can do it with small attacks.
You can destroy the men of a nation.
You must keep your campaign short.

8You must use total war, fighting with everything you have.
Never stop fighting when at war.
You can gain complete advantage.
To do this, you must plan your strategy of attack.

What happens when you go after an entrenched position?

You can try for that job, but you won't win it.

First, you must build a case against the current jobholder.

You need to find evidence and examples of problems.

This takes months, and your evidence still won't be accepted.

You then try to form a group of supporters.

After more months of work, you will make little progress.

You will get frustrated and angry.

You then attack the current jobholder directly.

This costs you more credibility.

You are still unable to dislodge him from his position.

This type of job-seeking is disastrous.

3 Build your career wisely.

Let people offer you more responsibility.

You can get responsibility without fighting for a new position.

You can go around people in entrenched roles.

You get a better job by getting small promotions.

You win away the responsibilities of others.

You must keep your goals well focused.

Concentrate on your career with all the skills at your disposal.

Everything you do matters.

You can win complete authority.

To do this, you must plan a strategy for advancement.

[12]The rules for making war are:
If you outnumber enemy forces ten to one, surround them.
If you outnumber them five to one, attack them.
If you outnumber them two to one, divide them.
If you are equal, then find an advantageous battle.
If you are fewer, defend against them.
If you are much weaker, evade them.

[19]Small forces are not powerful.
However, large forces cannot catch them.

You must master command. 4
The nation must support you.

[3]Supporting the military makes the nation powerful.
Not supporting the military makes the nation weak.

[5]The army's position is made more difficult by politicians in three different ways.
Ignorant of the whole army's inability to advance, they order an advance.
Ignorant of the whole army's inability to withdraw, they order a withdrawal.
We call this tying up the army.
Politicians don't understand the army's business.
Still, they think they can run an army.
This confuses the army's officers.

Here are the rules for building a career:
If you are already the boss, expand your operation.
If you are near the top, become more aggressive.
If you are further down, invent your own division.
If you are a low-level manager, outperform the others.
If you are an experienced employee, defend your rare skills.
If you are a new employee, develop a special skill.

New employees are not critical.
However, large companies cannot do without them.

4 You must be willing to manage.
Your organization will value you.

Promoting good people makes an organization successful.
Not promoting good people makes an organization weak.

Bad managers create problems for your career in three different ways.
Ignorant of your lack of resources, bad managers put you in a position to fail.
Ignorant of what you can accomplish, they hold you back from achievement.
This is hamstringing your efforts.
Poor managers don't understand your skills and goals.
They think they are helping your career.
This only confuses others.

[12]Politicians don't know the army's chain of command.
They give the army too much freedom.
This will create distrust among the army's officers.

[15]The entire army becomes confused and distrusting.
This invites invasion by many different rivals.
We say correctly that disorder in an army kills victory.

You must know five things to win: 5
Victory comes from knowing when to attack and when to avoid battle.
Victory comes from correctly using both large and small forces.
Victory comes from everyone sharing the same goals.
Victory comes from finding opportunities in problems.
Victory comes from having a capable commander and the government leaving him alone.
You must know these five things.
You then know the theory of victory.

We say: 6
"Know yourself and know your enemy.
You will be safe in every battle.
You may know yourself but not know the enemy.
You will then lose one battle for every one you win.
You may not know yourself or the enemy.
You will then lose every battle."

✦ ✦ ✦

Bad managers do not understand how to support you.
They don't make it clear what your responsiblities are.
This creates uncertainty in your career.

When responsibilities are confused, everyone is distrusting.
This invites internal political bickering.
Lack of clear goals destroys your chances of success.

5 You must know five things to advance your career:
Success comes from knowing when to make a change and when to
stay where you are.
Success comes from excelling at both the small and the large tasks
you are given.
Success comes from sharing your organization's goals.
Success comes from turning problems into opportunities.
Success comes from learning to manage and avoiding internal
politics.
You must know these five things.
You then know the philosophy of building a career.

6 Experience says this:
Know your abilities and your limitations.
If you do, you will be safe taking any new position.
You may know your abilities but not your limitations.
Then, for every successful position, you will fail in another.
You may know neither your abilities nor your limitations.
Then you will fail in every position.

✦ ✦ ✦

Related Articles from *Sun Tzu's Playbook*

In this third chapter, Sun Tzu introduces the basics of advancing into new areas. To learn the step-by-step techniques involved, we recommend the Sun Tzu's Art of War Playbook articles listed below.

1.1.1 Position Dynamics: how all current positions are always getting better or worse.

1.1.2 Defending Positions: how we defend our current positions until new positions are established.

1.2 Subobjective Positions: the subjective and objective aspects of a position.

1.3.1 Competitive Comparison: competition as the comparison of positions.

1.7 Competitive Power: the sources of superiority in challenges.

1.7.1 Team Unity: strength by joining with others.

1.7.2 Goal Focus: strength as arising from concentrating efforts.

1.8 Progress Cycle: the adaptive loop by which positions are advanced.

1.8.1 Creation and Destruction: the creation and destruction of competitive positions.

1.8.2 The Adaptive Loop: the continual reiteration of position analysis.

2.3.6 Promises and Threats: the use of promises and threats as strategic moves.

2.4 Contact Networks: the range of contacts needed to create perspective.

2.4.1 Ground Perspective: getting information on a new competitive arena.

2.4.2 Climate Perspective: getting perspective on temporary external conditions.

3.0.0 Identifying Opportunities: the use of opportunities to advance a position.

3.1.3 Conflict Cost: the costly nature of resolving competitive comparisons by conflict.

3.2 Opportunity Creation: how change creates opportunities.

3.2.2 Opportunity Invisibility: why opportunities are always hidden.

3.2.4 Emptiness and Fullness: the transformations between strength and weakness.

3.4 Dis-Economies of Scale: how opportunities are created by the size of others.

3.4.2 Opportunity Fit: finding new opportunities that fit your size.

3.4.3 Reaction Lag: how size creates temporary openings.

3.5 Strength and Weakness: openings created by the strength of others.

3.6 Leveraging Subjectivity: openings between subjective and objective positions.

3.7 Defining the Ground: redefining a competitive arena to create relative mismatches.

5.6 Defensive Advances: balancing defending and advancing positions.

Chapter 4

形

Positioning (Getting Promoted)

Sun Tzu's concept of positioning means moving to a new position *only* when an opportunity presents itself. As you move your career forward, positioning is the key to getting promoted easily.

Sun Tzu starts by explaining that you can do no more than protect your existing position; only the competitive environment itself can create new opportunities for you.

The text then explains that your success first depends on your ability to defend your current position.

It then explains that after you see an opportunity (foresight), you must be able to both move to the new position and take advantage of it when you get there.

Then Sun Tzu provides a simple formula for calculating whether or not you can succeed in winning a new position; this is done by calculating the relative balance of forces at the place and time of battle.

In the final section, Sun Tzu touches briefly on how critical positioning is in getting what you want out of the people with whom you work.

Positioning

SUN TZU SAID:

Learn from the history of successful battles. 1
Your first actions should deny victory to the enemy.
You pay attention to your enemy to find the way to win.
You alone can deny victory to the enemy.
Only your enemy can allow you to win.

[6]You must fight well.
You can prevent the enemy's victory.
You cannot win unless the enemy enables your victory.

[9]We say:
You see the opportunity for victory; you don't create it.

Getting Promoted

1 Learn from the history of successful people.
First, you must preserve your existing job.
You then pay attention to the job market to find advancement.
You alone can preserve your existing position.
Only others create a new opportunity for your advancement.

You must perform well.
You can prevent the loss of your existing job.
You cannot win a new job unless others need your services.

The truth is simple.
You must discover a new opportunity; you do not create it.

You are sometimes unable to win. 2
You must then defend.
You will eventually be able to win.
You must then attack.
Defend when you have insufficient strength.
Attack when you have a surplus of strength.

7You must defend yourself well.
Save your forces and dig in.
You must attack well.
Move your forces when you have a clear advantage.

11You must always protect yourself until you can completely triumph.

Some may see how to win. 3
However, they cannot position their forces where they must.
This demonstrates limited ability.

4Some can struggle to a victory and the whole world may praise their winning.
This also demonstrates a limited ability.

6Win as easily as picking up a fallen hair.
Don't use all of your forces.
See the time to move.
Don't try to find something clever.
Hear the clap of thunder.
Don't try to hear something subtle.

2 You cannot always advance to a new position.
You must then concentrate on your existing position.
You will eventually discover a better opportunity.
Then you must go after that position.
Stay in your current job when you are unqualified for advancement.
Go after a new position when you are more than qualified.

You must handle your existing responsibilities well.
Develop your experience and dig in.
You must campaign well for a new position.
Go after a better position as soon as you are qualified for it.

Keep developing experience until you are certain you can win advancement in the organization.

3 You may see a new position that you would like.
Yet you do not see how to qualify yourself for that position.
This shows limited ability.

You can sometimes win a better position for which you are poorly qualified.
This also shows limited ability.

Move into new positions of responsibility effortlessly.
Avoid risking your current job.
Watch for the right time to move.
Do not try to be too clever.
Learning about opportunities is easy if you listen.
Don't imagine opportunities where there are none.

[12]Learn from the history of successful battles.
Victory goes to those who make winning easy.
A good battle is one that you will obviously win.
It doesn't take intelligence to win a reputation.
It doesn't take courage to achieve success.

[17]You must win your battles without effort.
Avoid difficult struggles.
Fight when your position must win.
You always win by preventing your defeat.

[21]You must engage only in winning battles.
Position yourself where you cannot lose.
Never waste an opportunity to defeat your enemy.

[24]You win a war by first assuring yourself of victory.
Only afterward do you look for a fight.
Outmaneuver the enemy before the first battle and then
fight to win.

Learn from the successful careers of others.
Good jobs go to people who make promoting them easy.
A good position is one that you can obviously do well in.
It does not take a genius to develop a good reputation.
You do not have to take risks to advance your career.

You want to win a new position without effort.
Avoid highly competitive situations.
Go after a job when your experience will win it.
You get experience by developing your existing job.

You must court only valuable promotions.
Get the experience that makes you valuable.
Never pass by an opportunity to advance your career.

You win better jobs by developing skills and experience.
Only then do you search for more responsibilities.
Expand your current responsibilities before wanting a new position,
and then win that position.

You must make good use of war. 4
Study military philosophy and the art of defense.
You can control your victory or defeat.

[4]This is the art of war:
"1.   Discuss the distances.
2.   Discuss your numbers.
3.   Discuss your calculations.
4.   Discuss your decisions.
5.   Discuss victory.

[10]The ground determines the distance.
The distance determines your numbers.
Your numbers determine your calculations.
Your calculations determine your decisions.
Your decisions determine your victory."

[15]Creating a winning war is like balancing a coin of gold
against a coin of silver.
Creating a losing war is like balancing a coin of silver
against a coin of gold.

Winning a battle is always a matter of people. 5
You pour them into battle like a flood of water pouring into
a deep gorge.
This is a matter of positioning.

⁑ ⁑ ⁑

4 You must build your career carefully.
Study your industry and improve your performance.
You alone determine your success or failure.

Before you can take a new position, you must:
1.   Discuss the job's responsibilities.
2.   Discuss your qualifications.
3.   Discussion the job fit.
4.   Discuss the position's authority.
5.   Discuss your future advancement.

An employer's needs determine the job's responsibilities.
These responsibilities determine your qualifications.
Your qualifications determine the job fit.
The job fit determines the position's authority.
The job's authority determines your future advancement.

You want positions that offer you more future opportunities than your current position offers.
You don't want positions that offer fewer opportunities than your current position offers.

5 Winning advancement always depends on qualifications.
When you find the right new position, your qualifications should be undeniable.
This depends on your experience.

✦ ✦ ✦

Related Articles from *Sun Tzu's Playbook*

In this fourth chapter, Sun Tzu explains the process for advancing positions. To learn the step-by-step techniques involved, we recommend the Sun Tzu's Art of War Playbook *articles listed below.*

1.1.2 Defending Positions: how we defend our current positions until new positions are established.

1.2 Subobjective Positions: the subjective and objective aspects of a position.

1.3.1 Competitive Comparison: competition as the comparison of positions.

1.7 Competitive Power: the sources of superiority in challenges.

1.8 Progress Cycle: the adaptive loop by which positions are advanced.

1.8.1 Creation and Destruction: the creation and destruction of competitive positions.

1.8.2 The Adaptive Loop: the continual reiteration of position analysis.

3.0.0 Identifying Opportunities: the use of opportunities to advance a position.

3.2 Opportunity Creation: how change creates opportunities.

3.2.4 Emptiness and Fullness: the transformations between strength and weakness.

3.4.2 Opportunity Fit: finding new opportunities that fit your size.

3.5 Strength and Weakness: openings created by the strength of others.

3.7 Defining the Ground: redefining a competitive arena to create relative mismatches.

5.6 Defensive Advances: balancing defending and advancing positions.

5.6.1 Defense Priority: why defense has first claim on our resources.

9.4 Crisis Defense: how vulnerabilities are exploited and defended during a crisis.

9.4.1 Division Defense: preventing organizational division during a crisis.

9.4.2 Panic Defense: the mistakes arising from panic during a crisis.

9.4.3 Defending Openings: how to defend openings created by a crisis.

9.4.4 Defending Alliances: dealing with guilt by association.

9.4.5 Defensive Balance: using short-term conditions to tip the balance in a crisis.

Standards   Standards

⟵ Momentum ⟶

Surprise   Surprise

Chapter 5

势

Momentum (Career Momentum)

The central topic of this chapter is creativity. By using creative approaches with standard practices, you create what Sun Tzu calls *momentum*. Momentum in your career also depends upon your ability to find creative solutions to problems.

Sun Tzu begins by explaining that action—the combination of movement and position—can be either predictable or surprising.

He then explains that predictability and surprise, that is, innovation, depend on one another. There are an infinite number of paths to innovation. He uses the metaphors of music, color, and flavor to illustate this. These metaphors refer to knowledge, foresight, and positioning, respectively.

Sun Tzu then contrasts the ideas of momentum and timing. Momentum means building up pressure while timing releases it at the right time.

The text then addresses the chaotic nature of all competitive environments. Though you cannot eliminate this chaos, you can control it by planning your surprises or innovations at the right time.

In the final section, the pressure of momentum is explained in terms of its effect upon other people and their attitude.

Momentum

SUN TZU SAID:

You control a large group the same as you control a few. 1
You just divide their ranks correctly.
You fight a large army the same as you fight a small one.
You only need the right position and communication.
You may meet a large enemy army.
You must be able to sustain an enemy attack without being
defeated.
You must correctly use both surprise and direct action.
Your army's position must increase your strength.
Troops flanking an enemy can smash them like eggs.
You must correctly use both strength and weakness.

It is the same in all battles. 2
You use a direct approach to engage the enemy.
You use surprise to win.

4You must use surprise for a successful invasion.
Surprise is as infinite as the weather and land.
Surprise is as inexhaustible as the flow of a river.

Career Momentum

1 You handle large responsibilities the same as small ones.
You need only to organize your resources correctly.
Solving big problems is the same as solving small ones.
You need the right experience and communication skills.
You may meet difficult challenges.
You can confront any difficulty without failing in your
responsibility.
You need to use both creative and standard procedures.
Your experience will increase your ability.
Find a new perspective that eliminates the problem.
You must leverage both your strengths and weaknesses.

2 It is the same in all jobs.
You must use standard approaches to address the daily workload.
Use creative ideas to solve problems.

You must use creativity to succeed in your career.
There are an infinite number of new ideas.
Creativity utilizes the changes around you.

7You can be stopped and yet recover the initiative.
You must use your days and months correctly.

9If you are defeated, you can recover.
You must use the four seasons correctly.

11There are only a few notes in the scale.
Yet you can always rearrange them.
You can never hear every song of victory.

14There are only a few basic colors.
Yet you can always mix them.
You can never see all the shades of victory.

17There are only a few flavors.
Yet you can always blend them.
You can never taste all the flavors of victory.

20You fight with momentum.
There are only a few types of surprises and direct actions.
Yet you can always vary the ones you use.
There is no limit to the ways you can win.

24Surprise and direct action give birth to each other.
They are like a circle without end.
You cannot exhaust all their possible combinations!

Surging water flows together rapidly. 3
Its pressure washes away boulders.
This is momentum.

Yesterday's failure can become tomorrow's success.
You must make progress every day.

You can make mistakes and still recover.
You must learn to leverage changes over time.

There are only a few basic issues in any problem.
But you can look at these issues any number of ways.
You can always discover new ways to outflank a problem.

There are only a few basic responsibilities in any job.
Yet you can reprioritize them at any time.
You will never exhaust all the good ways to get the work done.

There are only a few measures of productivity.
Yet they can be blended in any number of ways.
You will never run out of valuable measurements you can take.

You build a career with momentum.
You can always use creative and standard procedures.
You can use them to continually change your approach.
There is no limit to the ways you can highlight your value.

Creativity and standard procedures each require the other.
Creativity leads to standards and standards to creativity.
Using both, you will never run out of good ideas.

3 Creative actions fix problems quickly.
Such success creates a strong sense of capability.
This is career momentum.

⁴A hawk suddenly strikes a bird.
Its contact alone kills the prey.
This is timing.

⁷You must fight only winning battles.
Your momentum must be overwhelming.
Your timing must be exact.

¹⁰Your momentum is like the tension of a bent crossbow.
Your timing is like the pulling of a trigger.

War is very complicated and confusing. 4
Battle is chaotic.
Nevertheless, you must not allow chaos.

⁴War is very sloppy and messy.
Positions turn around.
Nevertheless, you must never be defeated.

⁷Chaos gives birth to control.
Fear gives birth to courage.
Weakness gives birth to strength.

¹⁰You must control chaos.
This depends on your planning.
Your men must brave their fears.
This depends on their momentum.

¹⁴You have strengths and weaknesses.
These come from your position.

A successful person identifies more responsibilities.
Asking at the right time secures those responsibilities.
This is career timing.

You must be successful in your role.
Your career momentum must be noticeable.
Your career timing must be exact.

Success in your current job creates tension.
Asking for new responsibilities releases that tension.

4 The job market is always complicated and confusing.
Personnel management is always difficult.
You must make getting hired and promoted easy.

Job responsibilities are frequently unclear.
Roles are constantly changing.
Nevertheless, you must always make your contribution clear.

The job market's confusion requires clear qualifications.
The employer's fear of hiring demands your confidence.
The organization's needs require your abilities.

You must clarify what qualifications are needed.
This depends on your career planning.
Your confidence must overcome an employer's fears.
This depends on your career momentum.

You have both strengths and weaknesses.
They arise from your experience.

[16]You must force the enemy to move to your advantage.
Use your position.
The enemy must follow you.
Surrender a position.
The enemy must take it.
You can offer an advantage to move him.
You can use your men to move him.
You can use your strength to hold him.

You want a successful battle. 5
To do this, you must seek momentum.
Do not just demand a good fight from your people.
You must pick good people and then give them momentum.

[5]You must create momentum.
You create it with your men during battle.
This is comparable to rolling trees and stones.
Trees and stones roll because of their shape and weight.
Offer men safety and they will stay calm.
Endanger them and they will act.
Give them a place and they will hold.
Round them up and they will march.

[13]You make your men powerful in battle with momentum.
This should be like rolling round stones down over a high,
steep cliff.
Momentum is critical.

✦ ✦ ✦

You want employers to give you the positions you desire.
Use your experience.
Employers must want you.
Give them what they need.
Employers must meet you halfway.
You can offer a concession to help them hire you.
You can use your success to seek advancement.
You use your skills to keep your employer happy.

5 You want a successful career.
You need career momentum.
Do not simply demand recognition for your abilities.
Find a good employer and generate career momentum.

You must create momentum in your career.
You do this by doing more than your job requires.
Your responsibilities should flow together.
They should create an important and meaningful position.
Give employers confidence and they will stay with you.
Give them the fear that they might lose you and they will act.
Have them give you a position that will hold you.
Clarify your responsibilities so you can act.

You make abilities more valuable with career momentum.
Portray your career as success naturally following upon success.
Use that momentum.

♦ ♦ ♦

Related Articles from *Sun Tzu's Playbook*

In his fifth chapter, Sun Tzu explains the process for creating momentum. To learn the step-by-step techniques involved, we recommend the Sun Tzu's Art of War Playbook articles listed below.

1.2 Subobjective Positions: the subjective and objective aspects of a position.

7.0 Creating Momentum: how momentum requires creativity.

7.1 Order from Chaos: the value of chaos in creating competitive momentum.

7.1.1 Creating Surprise: creating surprise using our chaotic environment.

7.1.2 Momentum Psychology: the psychology of surprise.

7.1.3 Standards and Innovation: the methodology of creativity.

7.2 Standards First: the role of standards in creating connections with others.

7.2.1 Proven Methods: identifying and recognizing the limits of best practices.

7.2.2 Preparing Expectations: how we shape other people's expectations.

7.3 Strategic Innovation: a simple system for innovation.

7.3.1 Expected Elements: dividing processes and systems into components.

Chapter 6

虛 實

Weakness and Strength (Organizational Politics)

The two opposing and complementary concepts that are the topic of this chapter are difficult to translate. The first means weakness, but it also means poverty and emptiness. The second means strength, but also wealth and fullness. These concepts are useful in job advancement as they help you understand and control the forces of internal organizational politics.

Sun Tzu begins to clarify this complex idea by explaining that an army that arrives at an empty battlefield is naturally stronger than one that moves into an area occupied by other forces.

He then continues this idea by explaining that movement through empty terrain is speedier and that both attack and defense are easier when you are working against emptiness or weakness.

Sun Tzu then explains the need for stealth in moving into areas that are undefended.

He covers how to focus your strengths against the weaknesses in the opposition's formations by keeping your plans a secret.

Then he extends the discusion to consider how secrecy creates opportunities to exploit weakness.

Sun Tzu then summarizes weakness and strength by applying these concepts to planning, action, position, and battle.

In the final section, he explains how good strategy means following the path of least resistance.

Weakness and Strength

SUN TZU SAID:

Always arrive first to the empty battlefield to await the 1
enemy at your leisure.
After the battleground is occupied and you hurry to it,
fighting is more difficult.

3You want a successful battle.
Move your men, but not into opposing forces.

5You can make the enemy come to you.
Offer him an advantage.
You can make the enemy avoid coming to you.
Threaten him with danger.

9When the enemy is fresh, you can tire him.
When he is well fed, you can starve him.
When he is relaxed, you can move him.

Organizational Politics

1 You want the advantage of getting to a good company before others do.
Avoid moving to companies where rivals are entrenched in the best jobs.

You want a successful career.
You can change positions, but don't go where you have rivals.

You can make employers come to you.
Let them know you are interested.
You can avoid the jobs that you don't want.
Make it seem expensive to hire you.

If employers feel well-staffed, make them feel a lack.
If employers feel satisfied, make them hungry for more.
If employers feel comfortable, make them restless.

Leave any place without haste. 2
Hurry to where you are unexpected.
You can easily march hundreds of miles without tiring.
To do so, travel through areas that are deserted.
You must take whatever you attack.
Attack when there is no defense.
You must have walls to defend.
Defend where it is impossible to attack.

9Be skilled in attacking.
Give the enemy no idea where to defend.

11Be skillful in your defense.
Give the enemy no idea where to attack.

Be subtle! Be subtle! 3
Arrive without any clear formation.
Ghostly! Ghostly!
Arrive without a sound.
You must use all your skill to control the enemy's decisions.

6Advance where he can't defend.
Charge through his openings.
Withdraw where the enemy cannot chase you.
Move quickly so that he cannot catch you.

2 Never leave an existing job in a hurry.
Move to a new job when it is unexpected.
You can change to a completely different type of industry.
But that industry must be hungry for new people.
You must get the positions you try to win.
Go after employers that need your skills.
The jobs that you win must be easy to hold.
Get hired where it will be difficult to lose your job.

Be skilled in winning jobs.
Know what an employer's needs are.

Be skilled in keeping jobs.
Give employers no idea what your weaknesses are.

3 Keep your own counsel.
Don't go into a new job with a clear agenda.
You must be careful.
Don't make waves in a new position.
You must skillfully control employers' perceptions.

Look for promotion into an area in which your employer needs help.
Aggressively fill the job's responsibilities.
Make sure that problems don't overwhelm you.
Move up an organization's ranks quickly.

[10]Always pick your own battles.
The enemy can hide behind high walls and deep trenches.
Do not try to win by fighting him directly.
Instead, attack a place that he must recapture.
Avoid the battles that you don't want.
You can divide the ground and yet defend it.
Don't give the enemy anything to win.
Divert him by coming to where you defend.

Make other men take a position while you take none. 4
Then focus your forces where the enemy divides his forces.
Where you focus, you unite your forces.
When the enemy divides, he creates many small groups.
You want your large group to attack one of his small ones.
Then you have many men where the enemy has but a few.
Your larger force can overwhelm his smaller one.
Then go on to the next small enemy group.
You can take them one at a time.

You must keep the place that you have chosen as a 5
battleground a secret.
The enemy must not know.
Force the enemy to prepare his defense in many places.
You want the enemy to defend many places.
Then you can choose where to fight.
His forces will be weak there.

You must pick your internal battles.

Rivals can be well ensconced in entrenched positions.

You can't overcome them by direct confrontation.

Instead, question their performance, which they have to defend.

Avoid confrontations you don't want.

Divide responsibilities so that you can defend your area.

Don't leave rivals anything to win by attacking you.

Discourage rivals from getting involved in your affairs.

4 Make others express their ideas before you voice yours.
Concentrate your thinking on the gaps in their plans.

When you take a position of responsibility, bring people together.

Let rivals divide the organization into small groups.

Unite a large group against the interests of a few.

You want the interests of the organization on your side.

You can easily beat a rival's small clique.

You can then go on to the next rival's clique.

Tackle them one at a time.

5 If you want to oppose a specific idea, you must keep your plans
a secret.

Your rivals must never know.

Encourage them to defend all of their positions.

They must spread themselves too thin.

You can then choose the project to attack.

They will be weak there.

7If he reinforces his front lines, he depletes his rear.
If he reinforces his rear, he depletes his front.
If he reinforces his right flank, he depletes his left.
If he reinforces his left flank, he depletes his right.
Without knowing the place of attack, he cannot prepare.
Without knowing the right place, he will be weak everywhere.

13The enemy has weak points.
Prepare your men against them.
He has strong points.
Make his men prepare themselves against you.

You must know the battleground. 6
You must know the time of battle.
You can then travel a thousand miles and still win the battle.

4The enemy should not know the battleground.
He shouldn't know the time of battle.
His left flank will be unable to support his right.
His right will be unable to support his left.
His front lines will be unable to support his rear.
His rear will be unable to support his front.
His support is distant even if it is only ten miles away.
What unknown place can be close?

12You control the balance of forces.
The enemy may have many men but they are superfluous.
How can they help him to victory?

People get support for one pet project at the cost of another.
They increase the budget in one area by decreasing it in another.
They add people to one group by taking them from another.
They spend more time in one place by neglecting others.
No one has enough resources to do everything.
This creates weak points that can be identified.

Your rivals have weak points.
Prepare yourself to address them.
Rivals have strong points.
They will forget their strengths if they are worried about you.

6 You must know where your organization needs help.
You must know when acting will help it.
Even if the task is difficult, you can make it successful.

Your rivals must not know what tasks you plan.
They must never know when your tasks start.
Rivals cannot then line up opposition to you.
Rivals cannot then draw away support from your role.
Rivals cannot keep people from joining you.
They cannot distract you from focusing on your goals.
Rivals must be ignorant even of the tasks that affect them.
If they don't know your plans, how can they fight you?

You decide the balance of power when you pick a given task.
Your rivals may be powerful, but their ignorance disarms them.
How can their influence hurt you?

[15]We say:
You must let victory happen.

[17]The enemy may have many men.
You can still control him without a fight.

When you form your strategy, know the strengths and 7
weaknesses of your plan.
When you execute a plan, know how to manage both action
and inaction.
When you take a position, know the deadly and the winning
grounds.
When you enter into battle, know when you have too many
or too few men.

[5]Use your position as your war's centerpiece.
Arrive at the battle without a formation.
Don't take a position in advance.
Then even the best spies can't report it.
Even the wisest general cannot plan to counter you.
Take a position where you can triumph using superior numbers.
Keep opposing forces ignorant.
Everyone should learn your location after your position has
given you success.
No one should know how your location gives you a winning
position.
Make a successful battle one from which the enemy cannot
recover.
You must continually adjust your position to his position.

The truth is plain.

You must let yourself be successful.

Your opponents can be numerous.

You can still control them while avoiding a confrontation.

7 When you shape a career plan, know the strengths and weaknesses of your organization.

When you plan a task, know what needs to be done and what doesn't.

When you make a proposal, know what ideas will win and what will lose.

When you face rivals, know when you have support and when you do not.

Use your experience as your career's centerpiece.

Go into an organization without an agenda.

Avoid getting categorized.

Then even your rivals can't speak against you.

Even the most senior manager cannot oppose you.

Plan tasks that have broad support within the organization.

Keep your rivals in the dark.

Rivals should only learn about your responsibilities when your projects are successful.

Your rivals should never know how you were able to make your projects a success.

When you are successful, make sure that rivals cannot steal the credit from you.

When they change their responsibilities, adjust your plans.

Manage your military position like water. **8**
Water takes every shape.
It avoids the high and moves to the low.
Your war can take any shape.
It must avoid the strong and strike the weak.
Water follows the shape of the land that directs its flow.
Your forces follow the enemy who determines how you win.

[8]Make war without a standard approach.
Water has no consistent shape.
If you follow the enemy's shifts and changes, you can always
find a way to win.
We call this shadowing.

[12]Fight five different campaigns without a firm rule for victory.
Use all four seasons without a consistent position.
Your timing must be sudden.
A few weeks determine your failure or success.

8 You must remain available within your organization.
You must do whatever job needs to be done.
Avoid creating too high of expectations.
You can adapt to any conditions.
Look for problems that you can turn into successes.
Let the needs of the organization dictate your actions.
Your success comes from addressing those needs.

You must avoid rigid ideas about your career path.
A successful career can take any shape.
If you follow shifts and changes in your organization you can always succeed.
This is called shadowing.

In each new job, be open to a new approach.
Use the current trends to form your opinions.
You must act quickly.
The initial impression you make determines your success.

◆ ◆ ◆

Related Articles from *Sun Tzu's Playbook*

In chapter six, Sun Tzu explains how to find opportunities by leveraging opposites. To learn the step-by-step techniques involved, we recommend the Sun Tzu's Art of War Playbook articles listed below.

3.2.4 Emptiness and Fullness: rules on the transformations between emptiness and fullness.

3.2.5 Dynamic Reversal: how situations reverse themselves naturally.

3.5 Strength and Weakness: six rules regarding openings created by the strength of others.

3.6 Leveraging Subjectivity: openings between subjective and objective positions.

3.7 Defining the Ground: redefining a competitive arena to create relative mismatches.

3.8 Strategic Matrix Analysis: two-dimensional representations of strategic space.

4.7 Competitive Weakness: how certain opportunities can bring out our weaknesses.

4.7.1 Command Weaknesses: the character flaws of leaders and how to exploit them.

4.7.2 Group Weaknesses: organizational weakness and where groups fail.

6.7 Tailoring to Conditions: overcoming opposition using conditions in the environment.

6.7.1 Form Adjustments: adapting responses based on the form of the ground.

6.7.2 Size Adjustments: adapting responses based on comparing size of forces.

6.7.3 Strength Adjustments: adapting responses based on unity of opposing forces.

6.8 Competitive Psychology: improving competitive psychology even in adversity and failure.

6.8.1 Adversity and Creativity: how we use adversity to spark our creativity.

6.8.2 Strength in Adversity: using adversity to increase a group's unity and focus.

Chapter 7

軍 爭

Armed Conflict (Internal Conflict)

In this chapter, Sun Tzu warns against engaging in direct confrontations without a decisive advantage. The later part of the chapter covers techniques for succeeding in battles when they occur. In your career, you can use the lessons of the chapter to avoid internal conflict and, when conflicts are unavoidable, to come out on top in them.

Sun Tzu begins by explaining the dangers of battle and that it cannot be undertaken carelessly.

He then explains the disasters that occur when you rush into battle with the enemy without proper preparation.

His third section reemphasizes the need for deception, that is, controlling others' perceptions, in such confrontations.

Sun Tzu then discusses the need for improved methods of communication during these situations. Good communication is the primary key to winning all battles.

He then addresses the proper timing for making contact with the enemy in order to control the situation.

In the final section, Sun Tzu provides a short but critical list of rules for avoiding mistakes during contact with the enemy.

Armed Conflict

SUN TZU SAID:

Everyone uses the arts of war. 1
You accept orders from the government.
Then you assemble your army.
You organize your men and build camps.
You must avoid disasters from armed conflict.

[6]Seeking armed conflict can be disastrous.
Because of this, a detour can be the shortest path.
Because of this, problems can become opportunities.

[9]Use an indirect route as your highway.
Use the search for advantage to guide you.
When you fall behind, you must catch up.
When you get ahead, you must wait.
You must know the detour that most directly accomplishes
your plan.

[14]Undertake armed conflict when you have an advantage.
Seeking armed conflict for its own sake is dangerous.

Internal Conflict

1 Everyone wants to build his or her career.
You get responsibilities from your superiors.
Then you assemble your resources.
You organize your tasks and prioritize them.
You must then avoid problems caused by internal conflict.

Internal conflict is costly to your career.
Because of this, you must be willing to compromise.
You must turn potential conflicts into opportunities.

You must go out of your way to avoid conflict.
Let your search for success guide you.
If you fall behind in your tasks, you must catch up.
If you get too far ahead of schedule, you must wait.
You must find a way of fulfilling your mission without hurting others.

Seek to outshine others only when it will help your career.
It is foolish to get involved in conflict unnecessarily.

You can build up an army to fight for an advantage. 2
Then you won't catch the enemy.
You can force your army to go fight for an advantage.
Then you abandon your heavy supply wagons.

⁵You keep only your armor and hurry after the enemy.
You avoid stopping day or night.
You use many roads at the same time.
You go hundreds of miles to fight for an advantage.
Then the enemy catches your commanders and your army.
Your strong soldiers get there first.
Your weaker soldiers follow behind.
Using this approach, only one in ten will arrive.
You can try to go fifty miles to fight for an advantage.
Then your commanders and army will stumble.
Using this method, only half of your soldiers will make it.
You can try to go thirty miles to fight for an advantage.
Then only two out of three get there.

¹⁸If you make your army travel without good supply lines,
your army will die.
Without supplies and food, your army will die.
If you don't save the harvest, your army will die.

2 You think you can build up support to win an internal conflict. Then your rival will make you look foolish.

You can get caught up with the idea of beating a rival.

You then forget that you succeed as part of an organization.

You can try to protect yourself and prove a rival wrong.

You can work day and night.

You can try to cover all your bases.

You can make real progress trying to show up an opponent.

Then your rival finds a problem with you or your responsibilities.

Your progress is forgotten.

Your problems are what people see.

Only a small fraction of your efforts will be rewarded.

You can try changing your plan to oppose a rival.

You will then eventually make a mistake.

You will be only half as successful as you could be.

You may go a little out of your way to attack a rival.

It will cost you more than it is worth.

If you try to build a career without getting broad support, you will fail.

Without focusing your time and efforts, you will fail.

If you do not concentrate on your responsibilities, you will fail.

[21]Do not let any of your potential enemies know what you are planning.

Still, you must not hesitate to form alliances.

You must know the mountains and forests.

You must know where the obstructions are.

You must know where the marshes are.

If you don't, you cannot move the army.

If you don't, you must use local guides.

If you don't, you can't take advantage of the terrain.

You make war using a deceptive position. 3

If you use deception, then you can move.

Using deception, you can upset the enemy and change the situation.

You can move as quickly as the wind.

You can rise like the forest.

You can invade and plunder like fire.

You can stay as motionless as a mountain.

You can be as mysterious as the fog.

You can strike like sounding thunder.

[10]Divide your troops to plunder the villages.

When on open ground, dividing is an advantage.

Don't worry about organization; just move.

Be the first to find a new route that leads directly to a winning plan.

This is how you are successful at armed conflict.

Instead, you must keep quiet about what ideas and tasks you are planning.

You must stay close to your rivals.

You must know your organization.

You must know where the potential problems are.

You must know where you might get bogged down.

If you don't, you can't move ahead.

You must develop information sources.

If you don't, you won't get promoted within the organization.

3 You must disguise your intentions to win out over rivals.

Controlling people's perceptions, you can succeed.

Controlling people's perceptions, you can outpace rivals and win promotion.

You must work quickly and stay focused.

You must be noticed by superiors but overlooked by rivals.

You must generate value for your organization.

You must not attract unwanted attention.

You must keep quiet about your career plans.

You must quietly stand out from the crowd.

Use half your efforts to make your value clear.

When making good progress, take some time to advertise it.

Don't worry about others; just keep working.

Innovate and be the first to create a breakthrough success for your organization.

This is the how you are successful in internal contests.

Military experience says: 4
"You can speak, but you will not be heard.
You must use gongs and drums.
You cannot really see your forces just by looking.
You must use banners and flags."

6You must master gongs, drums, banners and flags.
Place people as a single unit where they can all see and hear.
You must unite them as one.
Then the brave cannot advance alone.
The fearful cannot withdraw alone.
You must force them to act as a group.

12In night battles, you must use numerous fires and drums.
In day battles, you must use many banners and flags.
You must position your people to control what they see and hear.

You control your army by controlling its morale. 5
As a general, you must be able to control emotions.

3In the morning, a person's energy is high.
During the day, it fades.
By evening, a person's thoughts turn to home.
You must use your troops wisely.
Avoid the enemy's high spirits.
Strike when his men are lazy and want to go home.
This is how you master energy.

4 Career experience teaches us this:
"You can be successful, but your success will be overlooked.
You must promote your success to get noticed.
Superiors cannot know your capabilities just by looking.
You must make your success interesting."

Use reporting and novelty to get your superiors' attention.
Make sure that your successes are generally known.
Use your success to bring the team together.
Do not try to take credit alone.
Give credit to everyone involved.
You want to be seen as acting in the best interests of the group.

If you are little known and physically distant, you advertise more.
If you are better known, you must still win attention.
You must consider what people at every level of the company see
and hear about you.

5 You control your career by considering people's feelings.
You must also control your emotions.

In the morning, people are busy.
During the day, their energy fades.
In the evening, people want to go home.
You must time your contacts wisely.
Avoid bothering people when they are busy.
Get their agreement when they want to go home.
This is how you make agreement easy.

¹⁰Use discipline to await the chaos of battle.
Keep relaxed to await a crisis.
This is how you master emotion.

¹³Stay close to home to await a distant enemy.
Stay comfortable to await the weary enemy.
Stay well fed to await the hungry enemy.
This is how you master power.

Don't entice the enemy when his ranks are orderly. 6
You must not attack when his formations are solid
This is how you master adaptation.

⁴You must follow these military rules.
Do not take a position facing the high ground.
Do not oppose those with their backs to the wall.
Do not follow those who pretend to flee.
Do not attack the enemy's strongest men.
Do not swallow the enemy's bait.
Do not block an army that is heading home.
Leave an escape outlet for a surrounded army.
Do not press a desperate foe.
This is how you use military skills.

✦ ✦ ✦

When internal problems arise, don't overreact.
Keep calm in every crisis.
This is how you master your own emotions.

Stay close to your duties, and critics will be frustrated.
Stay well prepared, and critics will be unprepared.
Stay within budget, and critics will have no ammunition.
This is how you master power.

6 Do not antagonize rivals when they are well prepared.
You must avoid any conflicts with rivals who are well connected.
This is how you master adapting.

You must follow these rules in your career:
Do not offer an opinion that contradicts your superiors.
Do not criticize without offering alternatives.
Do not follow those who have failed in the past.
Do not attack your rival's successes.
Do not believe everything you hear.
Do not create problems for others.
Leave every critic a way to save face.
Do not create unhappy coworkers.
This is the art of building a career.

✦ ✦ ✦

Related Articles from *Sun Tzu's Playbook*

In chapter seven, Sun Tzu teaches us to focus on building positions instead of on tearing down opponents. To learn the step-by-step techniques involved, we recommend the Sun Tzu's Art of War Playbook *articles listed below.*

1.2.1 Competitive Landscapes: the arenas in which rivals jockey for position.

1.3.1 Competitive Comparison: competition as the comparison of positions.

1.5 Competing Agents: characteristics of competitors.

1.7 Competitive Power: the sources of superiority in challenges.

1.8.1 Creation and Destruction: the creation and destruction of competitive positions.

1.9 Competition and Production: the two opposing skill sets of competition and production.

2.1.3 Strategic Deception: misinformation and disinformation in competition.

2.6 Knowledge Leverage: getting competitive value out of knowledge.

2.7 Information Secrecy: the role of secrecy in relationships.

3.1 Strategic Economics: balancing the cost and benefits of positioning.

3.1.1 Resource Limitations: the inherent limitation of strategic resources.

3.1.3 Conflict Cost : the costly nature of resolving competitive comparisons by conflict.

3.1.6 Time Limitations: understanding the time limits on opportunities.

3.7 Defining the Ground: redefining a competitive arena to create relative mismatches.

4.7 Competitive Weakness: how certain opportunities can bring out our weaknesses.

6.1.2 Prioritizing Conditions: parsing complex competitive conditions into simple responses.

6.8 Competitive Psychology: improving competitive psychology even in adversity and failure.

7.4 Competitive Timing: the role of timing in creating momentum.

7.6 Productive Competition: using momentum to produce more resources.

7.6.2 Ground Creation: the creation of new competitive ground to be successful.

8.5 Leveraging Emotions: how we use emotion to obtain rewards.

9.5.2 Avoiding Emotion: the danger of exploiting environmental vulnerabilities for purely emotion reasons.

Chapter 8

九變

Adaptability (Flexibility in Your Career)

The topic of this chapter is the need to continually change your plans based upon changing conditions. In Sun Tzu's view, successful strategies must be dynamic. Although you want to develop special skills in your career, this chapter advises you not to be too rigid in thinking about how you can utilize those skills.

In the chapter's first section, Sun Tzu lists situations (covered in greater detail in several other chapters) that show the need to constantly change your plans.

The next short section makes the point that you can be creative and constantly adapt your methods without being inconsistent in your results.

The third section, also short, explains that you can use the dynamics of competitive situations to control your opponents' behavior.

Sun Tzu then covers the need to address the unpredictability of opponents in planning the defense of your position.

Finally, he lists the five weaknesses of leaders and explains how easily these weaknesses can be exploited in the dynamics of competition.

Adaptability

SUN TZU SAID:

Everyone uses the arts of war. 1
As a general, you get your orders from the government.
You gather your troops.
On dangerous ground, you must not camp.
Where the roads intersect, you must join your allies.
When an area is cut off, you must not delay in it.
When you are surrounded, you must scheme.
In a life-or-death situation, you must fight.
There are roads that you must not take.
There are armies that you must not fight.
There are strongholds that you must not attack.
There are positions that you must not defend.
There are government commands that must not be obeyed.

[14]Military leaders must be experts in knowing how to adapt
to find an advantage.
This will teach you the use of war.

[16]Some commanders are not good at making adjustments to
find an advantage.
They can know the shape of the terrain.
Still, they cannot find an advantageous position.

Flexibility in Your Career

1 These are basic rules of building a career.
You get direction from your superiors.
Then you organize your resources.
In difficult situations, you must not become too comfortable.
Where interests intersect, you must find allies.
If a job is a dead end, you must avoid it.
If you feel hemmed in, you must be creative.
When you are in a do-or-die situation, you must perform.
There are career paths that you must avoid.
There are political battles that you must not fight.
There are entrenched positions that you cannot win.
There are positions in which you cannot succeed.
There are bosses' instructions that you must ignore.

You must become an expert at knowing how to adapt to advance
your career.
Adaptation is the key to success.

Some people are unable to adapt their viewpoint to find a new
opportunity.
They can understand the changing job market.
Still, they cannot see their opportunity in it.

[19]Some military commanders do not know how to adjust
their methods.
They can find an advantageous position.
Still, they cannot use their men effectively.

You must be creative in your planning. 2
You must adapt to your opportunities and weaknesses.
You can use a variety of approaches and still have a
consistent result.
You must adjust to a variety of problems and consistently
solve them.

You can deter your potential enemy by using his 3
weaknesses against him.
You can keep your potential enemy's army busy by giving it
work to do.
You can rush your potential enemy by offering him an
advantageous position.

You must make use of war. 4
Do not trust that the enemy isn't coming.
Trust your readiness to meet him.
Do not trust that the enemy won't attack.
Rely only on your ability to pick a place that the enemy can't
attack.

Some people are unable to adapt their experience to fit a desired job.

They can see a good opportunity in the market.

Still, they cannot qualify themselves for it.

2 You must be inventive in advancing your career.

You must adapt to your opportunities and challenges.

You can use different approaches and still consistently move your career forward.

You can face a variety of problems and consistently find a way to solve them.

3 You can win any position by using the employer's needs to leverage him.

You must interest an employer by giving him an opportunity to think about.

You can hasten the decision by offering the employer a reason to decide now.

4 You must always be working on your career.

Do not think that you don't have an opportunity to advance.

Instead, be ready to meet the opportunity should it arise.

Do not trust that your current position is safe.

Instead, work to make yourself indispensable in your current position.

You can exploit five different faults in a leader. 5
If he is willing to die, you can kill him.
If he wants to survive, you can capture him.
He may have a quick temper.
You can then provoke him with insults.
If he has a delicate sense of honor, you can disgrace him.
If he loves his people, you can create problems for him.
In every situation, look for these five weaknesses.
They are common faults in commanders.
They always lead to military disaster.

[11]To overturn an army, you must kill its general.
To do this, you must use these five weaknesses.
You must always look for them.

5 You can use five different weaknesses in a superior.
If a superior is willing to be replaced, you can replace him.
If he wants to stay where he is, you can get his support.
Some superiors overreact.
You can manipulate their emotions.
If a superior is honorable, you make him indebted to you.
If he cares for his people, you can become his protégé.
In every situation, look for these five characteristics.
Look for these characteristics in your supervisors.
They can help you avoid career disaster.

Advancing in some organizations means replacing your boss.
You must know how to exploit his weaknesses.
You must always be aware of them.

♦ ♦ ♦

Related Articles from *Sun Tzu's Playbook*

In chapter eight, Sun Tzu teaches us the need to constantly adapt to the situation. To learn the step-by-step techniques involved, we recommend the Sun Tzu's Art of War Playbook *articles listed below.*

1.8 Progress Cycle: the adaptive loop by which positions are advanced.

1.8.1 Creation and Destruction : the creation and destruction of competitive positions.

1.8.2 The Adaptive Loop: the continual reiteration of position analysis.

1.8.3 Cycle Time: the importance of speed in feedback and reaction.

1.8.4 Probabilistic Process: the role of chance in strategic processes and systems.

4.7.1 Command Weaknesses: the character flaws of leaders and how to exploit them.

5.2.1 Choosing Adaptability: choosing actions that allow us a maximum of future flexibility.

5.2.2 Campaign Methods: the use of campaigns and their methods.

5.2.3 Unplanned Steps: distinguishing campaign adjustments from steps in a plan.

5.3 Reaction Time: the use of speed in choosing actions.

5.3.1 Speed and Quickness: the use of pace within a dynamic environment.

6.0 Situation Response: selecting the actions most appropriate to a situation.

6.1 Situation Recognition: situation recognition in making advances.

6.1.1 Conditioned Reflexes: how we develop automatic, instantaneous responses.

6.1.2 Prioritizing Conditions: parsing complex competitive conditions into simple responses.

6.2 Campaign Evaluation: how we justify continued investment in an ongoing campaign.

6.2.1 Campaign Flow: seeing campaigns as a series of situations that flow logically from one to another.

6.2.2 Campaign Goals: assessing the value of a campaign by a larger mission.

6.3 Campaign Patterns: how knowing campaign stages gives us insight into our situation.

6.5 Nine Responses: the best responses to the nine common competitive situations.

6.7 Tailoring to Conditions: overcoming opposition using conditions in the environment.

6.7.1 Form Adjustments: adapting our responses based on the form of the ground.

6.7.2 Size Adjustments: adapting responses based on the relative size of opposing forces.

6.7.3 Strength Adjustments: how to adapt responses based on the relative strength of opposing missions.

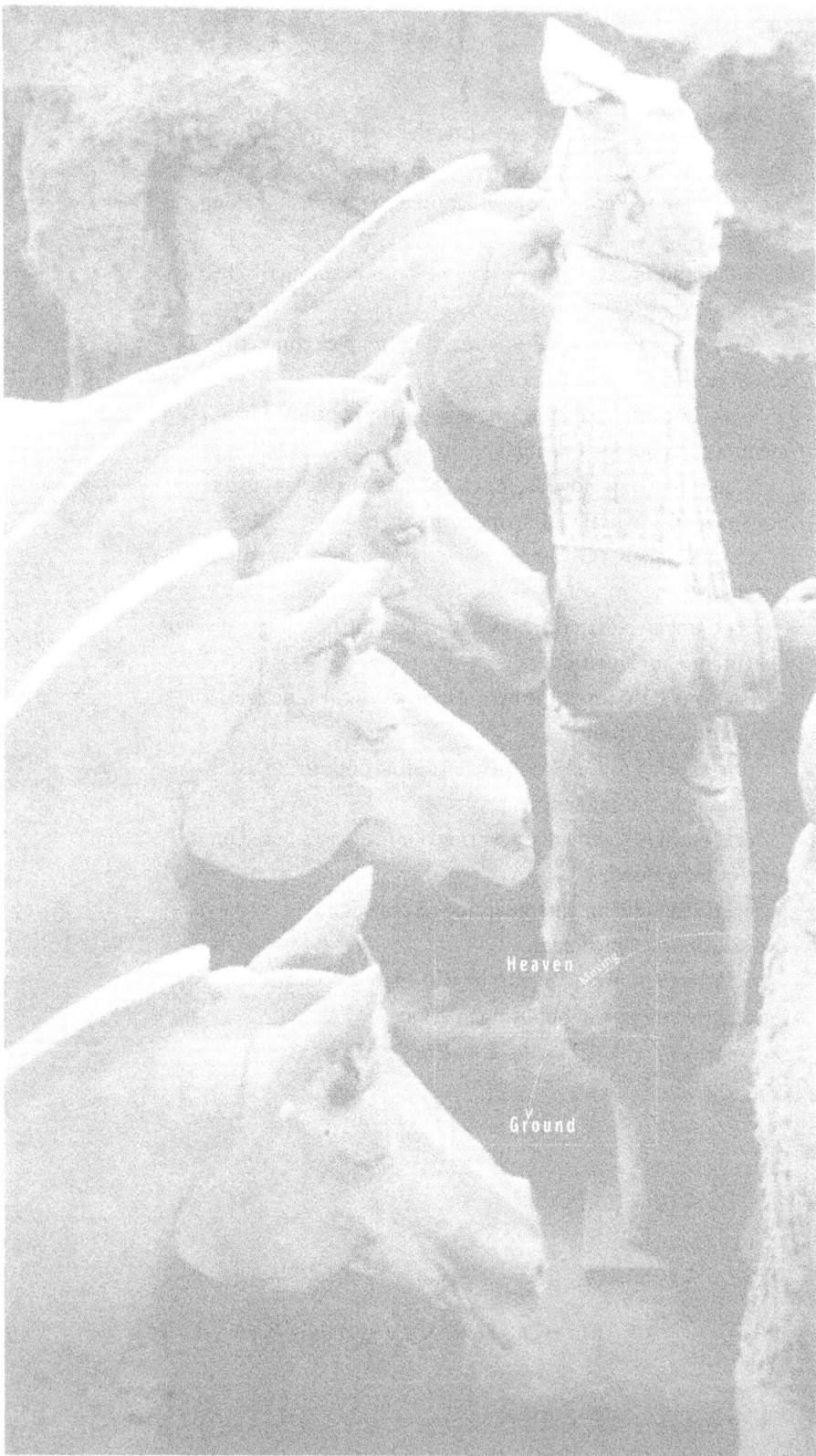

Heaven

Ground

Chapter 9

行軍

Armed March (Your Job Search)

This long chapter addresses the challenges encountered when moving an organization into new competitive territory. Much of it is dedicated to correctly interpreting signs in the environment. For you as a job hunter, this chapter serves as a guide to searching out the best possible place for your skills.

The chapter's first section covers four different categories of territory and how to navigate them.

Sun Tzu then briefly addresses the need to control the high ground in whatever type of situation you encounter.

He then warns about the seasonal and hidden dangers inherent in exploring new territory.

He then spends some time explaining various signs in the environment and how to interpret them.

In the long fifth section, Sun Tzu explains in detail how you can determine the conditions and intentions of your opponents by interpreting their behavior.

Sun Tzu ends the chapter by describing how to know when you have gone as far as you can go in a new competitive arena and how you can regroup.

Armed March

Sun Tzu said:

Anyone moving an army must adjust to the enemy. 1
When caught in the mountains, rely on their valleys.
Position yourself on the heights facing the sun.
To win your battles, never attack uphill.
This is how you position your army in the mountains.

6When water blocks you, keep far away from it.
Let the invader cross the river and wait for him.
Do not meet him in midstream.
Wait for him to get half his forces across and then take
advantage of the situation.

10You need to be able to fight.
You can't do that if you are caught in water when you meet
an invader.
Position yourself upstream, facing the sun.
Never face against the current.
Always position your army upstream when near the water.

Your Job Search

1 In interviewing for new jobs, you must adjust to your situation.
Working in large organizations is harder than working in small ones.
Interview with large organizations for responsible, visible roles.
To be successful, respect the organization's hierarchy.
This is how to build a career in a large organization.

If reorganization blocks your job search, distance yourself from it.
Let others get involved with reorganization.
Do not look for new positions during this type of change.
Wait to see what happens to see if you can take advantage of the
situation.

You need to perform successfully where you are.
You can't be successful if you are weeded out in an internal
reorganization.
Position yourself visibly in an organization's future.
Never fight against organizational trends.
Position yourself with the trends during an internal reorganization.

¹⁵You may have to move across marshes.
Move through them quickly without stopping.
You may meet the enemy in the middle of a marsh.
You must keep on the water grasses.
Keep your back to a clump of trees.
This is how you position your army in a marsh.

²¹On a level plateau, take a position that you can change.
Keep the higher ground on your right and to the rear.
Keep danger in front of you and safety behind.
This is how you position yourself on a level plateau.

²⁵You can find an advantage in all four of these situations.
Learn from the great emperor who used positioning to
conquer his four rivals.

Armies are stronger on high ground and weaker on low. 2
They are better camping on sunny southern hillsides than
on shady northern ones.
Provide for your army's health and place men correctly.
Your army will be free from disease.
Done correctly, this means victory.

⁶You must sometimes defend on a hill or riverbank.
You must keep on the south side in the sun.
Keep the uphill slope at your right rear.

⁹This will give the advantage to your army.
It will always give you a position of strength.

Your career path may take you into temporary jobs.
Get out of these positions as quickly as you can.
You may meet challenges in a temporary position.
Ally yourself with the long-term employees of the organization.
Defend your role and your value.
This is how you manage your career in a temporary job.

When interviewing with flat organizations, keep yourself flexible.
Make yourself visible and keep the management with you.
Face challenges directly and defend your actions.
This is how you manage a career in a flat organization.

You can find opportunities in any type of job.
Learn from the success of people who discover opportunities
whereever they are.

2 Jobs that require rare skills are more stable than those that do not.
You are better off seeking a visible, active role rather than a quiet,
hidden one.
Keep your career healthy; look only for valuable positions.
The positions should not hinder your ability.
Do this correctly and you will be successful.

Sometimes you defend a job you've held or a change you've made.
Highlight the value of your experience.
Have your past supervisors support you.

This will highlight your breadth of experience.
This will always give you a position of strength.

Stop the march when the rain swells the river into rapids. 3
You may want to ford the river.
Wait until it subsides.

4All regions can have seasonal mountain streams that can
cut you off.
There are seasonal lakes.
There are seasonal blockages.
There are seasonal jungles.
There are seasonal floods.
There are seasonal fissures.
Get away from all these quickly.
Do not get close to them.
Keep them at a distance.
Maneuver the enemy close to them.
Position yourself facing these dangers.
Push the enemy back into them.

16Danger can hide on your army's flank.
There are reservoirs and lakes.
There are reeds and thickets.
There are mountain woods.
Their dense vegetation provides a hiding place.
You must cautiously search through them.
They can always hide an ambush.

3 Stop seeking a new job during big change in your industry.
You want to survive any transition.
Wait until the changes subside.

All organizations have positions that are dead ends with no chance
of promotion.
There are roles that are difficult to succeed in.
There are positions that are too highly paid.
There are positions that no one sees.
There are projects that are doomed to fail.
There are jobs that offer no advancement.
Do not go after these positions.
Never accept them.
Don't let them become a bottleneck for your career.
Let your rivals in the job market fight for them.
Identify these positions within your target organization.
Suggest the qualifications others need to fill them.

Your career can be blindsided.
Beware of a potential employer's habits and prejudices.
Beware of making false assumptions about employers.
Beware of well-established internal rivals.
The entrenched can be the basis for unpleasant surprises.
You must take time to learn about a potential employer.
Don't be taken unawares.

Sometimes, the enemy is close by but remains calm. 4
Expect to find him in a natural stronghold.
Other times he remains at a distance but provokes battle.
He wants you to attack him.

5He sometimes shifts the position of his camp.
He is looking for an advantageous position.

7The trees in the forest move.
Expect that the enemy is coming.
The tall grasses obstruct your view.
Be suspicious.

11The birds take flight.
Expect that the enemy is hiding.
Animals startle.
Expect an ambush.

15Notice the dust.
It sometimes rises high in a straight line.
Vehicles are coming.
The dust appears low in a wide band.
Foot soldiers are coming.
The dust seems scattered in different areas.
The enemy is collecting firewood.
Any dust is light and settling down.
The enemy is setting up camp.

4 A potential employer seems interested but is quiet.
You should expect that he is well staffed.
Another possible employer seems distant but keeps in contact.
He wants you to sell yourself to him.

A potential employer changes the benefits that he offers.
He sees hiring you as an opportunity.

You hear of opportunities in the job market.
Expect that an employer is active.
People are keeping secrets from you.
Be suspicious.

Your calls about a job are not returned.
Suspect that an employer is delaying.
Contacts are nervous.
A rival is undercutting you.

Pay attention to rumors about being hired.
A rumor can come straight from top management.
Expect a quick job offer.
A rumor seems to be common knowledge.
Expect communication from a potential employer.
The rumor seems to be scattered here and there.
The potential employer is thinking about waiting.
Rumors become rarer and rarer.
The potential employer is stalling.

Your enemy speaks humbly while building up forces. 5
He is planning to advance.

³The enemy talks aggressively and pushes as if to advance.
He is planning to retreat.

⁵Small vehicles exit his camp first.
They move the army's flanks.
They are forming a battle line.

⁸Your enemy tries to sue for peace but without offering a
treaty.
He is plotting.

¹⁰Your enemy's men run to leave and yet form ranks.
You should expect action.

¹²Half his army advances and the other half retreats.
He is luring you.

¹⁴Your enemy plans to fight but his men just stand there.
They are starving.

¹⁶Those who draw water drink it first.
They are thirsty.

¹⁸Your enemy sees an advantage but does not advance.
His men are tired.

5 A potential employer speaks humbly and improves his offer.
He is planning to win you.

A potential employer aggressively demands a decision.
He is going to withdraw his offer.

A potential employer gets tired of waiting and puts a deadline on your decision.
He has had enough.

A potential employer asks you to stay but doesn't make a concrete offer.
He is plotting.

A potential employer claims disinterest but counters an offer.
Expect him to come back again.

A potential employer gives in to half of your demands.
He is tempting you.

A potential employer plans to hire you but makes no offer.
He is out of resources.

An employer is concerned about when to pay you.
He is short of money.

A potential employer is busy despite his lack of growth.
His people are overworked.

²⁰Birds gather.
Your enemy has abandoned his camp.

²²Your enemy's soldiers call in the night.
They are afraid.

²⁴Your enemy's army is raucous.
The men do not take their commander seriously.

²⁶Your enemy's banners and flags shift.
Order is breaking down.

²⁸Your enemy's officers are irritable.
They are exhausted.

³⁰Your enemy's men kill their horses for meat.
They are out of provisions.

³²They don't put their pots away or return to their tents.
They are desperate.

³⁴Enemy troops appear sincere and agreeable.
But their men are slow to speak to each other.
They are no longer united.

³⁷Your enemy offers too many incentives to his men.
He is in trouble.

³⁹Your enemy gives out too many punishments.
His men are weary.

The phone isn't answered.
A potential employer has gone out of business.

A potential employer's people secretly complain.
They are unhappy.

A potential employer's people are undisciplined.
They don't take their organization's management seriously.

A potential employer is going through reorganization.
The structure is breaking down.

A potential employer's managers are irritable.
These managers are stretched thin.

A potential employer is selling off part of his business.
He is short of funds.

A potential employer's key people are leaving.
These key people expect the organization to fail.

A potential employer's people are polite with one another.
However, these people communicate poorly.
They lack a common goal.

A potential employer offers too much compensation.
His organization is in trouble.

A potential employer is strict about meeting quotas.
He is under pressure.

41Your enemy first acts violently and then is afraid of your
larger force.
His best troops have not arrived.

43Your enemy comes in a conciliatory manner.
He needs to rest and recuperate.

45Your enemy is angry and appears to welcome battle.
This goes on for a long time, but he doesn't attack.
He also doesn't leave the field.
You must watch him carefully.

If you are too weak to fight, you must find more men. 6
In this situation, you must not act aggressively.
You must unite your forces.
Prepare for the enemy.
Recruit men and stay where you are.

6You must be cautious about making plans and adjust to the
enemy.
You must gather more men.

A potential employer first actively courts you but then seems afraid to hire you.

He needs approval.

A potential employer comes offering more responsibility.

He needs your help.

A potential employer is emotional and appears to want you.

The interview process goes on and on without an offer.

He remains in contact.

You must maintain your interest.

6 If you lack qualifications, you need more experience.

In this situation, don't seek new jobs aggressively.

You must focus your efforts.

You develop your skills.

You get experience and take your time.

You must change jobs carefully and adjust to the needs in the job market.

You must gain more experience.

With new, undedicated soldiers, you can depend on 7
them if you discipline them.
They will tend to disobey your orders.
If they do not obey your orders, they will be useless.

4You can depend on seasoned, dedicated soldiers.
But you must avoid disciplining them without reason.
Otherwise, you cannot use them.

7You must control your soldiers with esprit de corps.
You must bring them together by winning victories.
You must get them to believe in you.

10Make it easy for people to know what to do by training
your people.
Your people will then obey you.
If you do not make it easy for people to know what to do,
you won't train your people.
Then they will not obey.

14Make your commands easy to follow.
You must understand the way a crowd thinks.

♦ ♦ ♦

7 You can interview for jobs that demand new, untested skills if you are disciplined.
If you are not disciplined, you will make mistakes.
If you make mistakes, winning those jobs will be of no value.

It is different when depending on well-established, proven skills.
When you are skilled, you can interview for new roles comfortably.
Experience allows you to try new roles.

When interviewing for a job, you must be enthusiastic.
You must win people over by sharing your past success.
You must get them to believe in you.

Make it easy for people to believe in you by communicating with them clearly.
They will then trust you.
If you do not communicate well, people will not know how to react to you.
They will not trust you.

Make yourself easy to understand.
You must also understand how other employers think.

✦ ✦ ✦

Related Articles from *Sun Tzu's Playbook*

In chapter nine, Sun Tzu discusses the basics of recognizing conditions in new territory. To learn the step-by-step techniques involved, we recommend the Sun Tzu's Art of War Playbook *articles listed below.*

1.1.0 Position Paths: the continuity of strategic positions over time.

1.2.2 Exploiting Exploration: how competitive landscapes are searched and positions utilized.

2.1 Information Value: knowledge and communication as the basis of strategy.

2.1.1 Information Limits: making good decisions with limited information.

2.2.1 Personal Relationships: why information depends on personal relationships.

2.2.2 Mental Models: how mental models simplify decision-making.

2.2.3 Standard Terminology: how mental models must be shared to enable communication.

2.3 Personal Interactions: making progress through personal interactions.

2.3.1 Action and Reaction: how we advance based on how others react to our actions.

2.3.2 Reaction Unpredictability: why we can never exactly predict the reactions of others.

2.3.3 Likely Reactions: the range of potential reactions in gathering information.

2.3.4 Using Questions: using questions in gathering information and predicting reactions.

4.0 Leveraging Probability: making better decisions regarding our choice of opportunities.

4.3 Leveraging Form: how we can leverage the form of our territory.

4.3.1 Tilted Forms: opportunities that are dominated by uneven forces.

4.3.2 Fluid Forms: opportunities that are dominated by fast-changing directional forces.

4.3.3 Soft Forms: opportunities that are dominated by forces that create uncertainty.

4.3.4 Neutral Forms: opportunities where the terrain has no dominant forces.

4.4 Strategic Distance: relative proximity in strategic space.

4.4.1 Physical Distance: the issues of proximity in physical space.

4.4.2 Intellectual Distance: the challenges of moving through intellectual space.

Downloaded from
SEE PROFILE

Barricaded

Chapter 10

地 形

Field Position (Evaluating Opportunities)

This chapter examines in detail the six characteristics, called field positions, which can be used to evaluate your position, especially in terms of moving to a new position. As you manage your professional career, these characteristics help you analyze the available opportunities and judge their viability as stepping stones to better positions in the future.

Sun Tzu begins with a detailed description of the six types of field positions and how to utilize them.

He then lists the six flaws in organizations and how to diagnose them. Though it is not explained specifically in the text, each of these six flaws arises in and is amplified by the specific field position that corresponds to the order in which it is listed.

Sun Tzu then examines the issues that you must consider in moving from one temporary position to another.

He then addresses the proper way of providing leadership to your people as you lead them into new situations.

In the final section, Sun Tzu addresses the need to compare your relative field position with that of your opponent before choosing a course of action.

Field Position

SUN TZU SAID:

Some field positions are unobstructed. 1
Some field positions are entangling.
Some field positions are supporting.
Some field positions are constricted.
Some field positions give you a barricade.
Some field positions are spread out.

7You can attack from some positions easily.
Other forces can meet you easily as well.
We call these unobstructed positions.
These positions are open.
On them, be the first to occupy a high, sunny area.
Put yourself where you can defend your supply routes.
Then you will have an advantage.

Evaluating Opportunities

1 Some jobs are without barriers.
Some jobs are risky.
Some jobs are entrenched.
Some jobs are exclusive.
Some jobs are easy to protect.
Some jobs are spread too thin.

You can move up from some jobs easily.
Rivals can move up from these positions easily as well.
These are unobstructed positions.
These jobs offer no barriers to advancement.
In these jobs, seek visibility.
Put yourself in a position where you can protect your back.
Then these jobs offer an opportunity.

¹⁴You can attack from some positions easily.
Disaster arises when you try to return to them.
These are entangling positions.
These field positions are one-sided.
Wait until your enemy is unprepared.
You can then attack from these positions and win.
Avoid a well-prepared enemy.
You will try to attack and lose.
Since you can't return, you will meet disaster.
These field positions offer no advantage.

²⁴You cannot leave some positions without losing an
advantage.
If the enemy leaves this ground, he also loses an advantage.
We call these supporting field positions.
These positions strengthen you.
The enemy may try to entice you away.
Still, hold your position.
You must entice the enemy to leave.
You then strike him as he is leaving.
These field positions offer an advantage.

³³Some field positions are constricted.
Get to these positions first.
You must fill these areas and await the enemy.
Sometimes, the enemy will reach them first.
If he fills them, do not follow him.
However, if he fails to fill them, you can go after him.

You can move up from some jobs easily.
You cannot get back into these positions after leaving them.
These are risky jobs.
They give you one chance.
Wait until you are prepared to move up.
You can then move from risky positions into new ones.
Avoid moving from these jobs if you aren't ready.
You can win a promotion but then fail in the new position.
If you can't go back to your old job, you are unemployed.
These jobs offer no real opportunity.

You cannot leave some positions without passing up an
opportunity.
Anyone in this position is going to do well in the future.
This is a job in which you are entrenched.
Know when you should be entrenched in your job.
A rival may try to lure you away.
You must hold your position.
If a rival is entrenched, try to lure him away.
You can then go after his job.
Entrenched jobs offer a long-term opportunity.

Some jobs are exclusive.
You must get into these positions before rivals do.
You must perform well in these jobs and keep them.
A rival may get into one of these positions first.
If he performs well, don't try to follow him.
If he fails to perform, you can try to displace him.

39Some field positions give you a barricade.
Get to these positions first.
You must occupy their southern, sunny heights in order to
await the enemy.
Sometimes the enemy occupies these areas first.
If so, entice him away.
Never go after him.

45Some field positions are too spread out.
Your force may seem equal to the enemy.
Still you will lose if you provoke a battle.
If you fight, you will not have any advantage.

49These are the six types of field positions.
Each battleground has its own rules.
As a commander, you must know where to go.
You must examine each position closely.

Some armies can be outmaneuvered. 2
Some armies are too lax.
Some armies fall down.
Some armies fall apart.
Some armies are disorganized.
Some armies must retreat.

7Know all six of these weaknesses.
They create weak timing and disastrous positions.
They all arise from the army's commander.

Some jobs are easy to protect.
You must win these positions before rivals do.
You must then make yourself visible and wait for rivals to criticize you.
Sometimes rivals win these jobs first.
If so, they can only be tempted away.
Never criticize people in these positions.

Some jobs are spread too thin.
They may seem to offer an opportunity.
Nevertheless, you will never be successful in them.
These jobs offer no real opportunity.

Thus, there are six types of job opportunities.
Each type of job has its own rules.
To build a career, you must know which jobs to accept.
You must analyze each position carefully.

2 Some organizations are inflexible.
Some organizations are too lax.
Some organizations stumble.
Some organizations self-destruct.
Some organizations are chaotic.
Some organizations are shrinking.

You must recognize these six weaknesses.
These organizational problems affect your success.
These weaknesses come from the organization's leader.

¹⁰One general can command a force equal to the enemy.
Still his enemy outflanks him.
This means that his army can be outmaneuvered.

¹³Another can have strong soldiers but weak officers.
This means that his army is too lax.

¹⁵Another has strong officers but weak soldiers.
This means that his army will fall down.

¹⁷Another has subcommanders that are angry and defiant.
They attack the enemy and fight their own battles.
The commander cannot know the battlefield.
This means that his army will fall apart.

²¹Another general is weak and easygoing.
He fails to make his orders clear.
His officers and men lack direction.
This shows in his military formations.
This means that his army is disorganized.

²⁶Another general fails to predict the enemy.
He pits his small forces against larger ones.
His weak forces attack stronger ones.
He fails to pick his fights correctly.
This means that his army must retreat.

Organizations can look competitive on the outside.
Still, competitors lead the industry.
This means that these organizations are inflexible.

Organizations can have good managers but poor workers.
These organizations are too lax.

Organizations can have good workers but poor managers.
These organizations will stumble.

The organization's managers have their own priorities.
They want to fight each other over resources.
The organization's leader does not understand the politics.
This means that the organization will self-destruct.

Some organizations' leaders are lazy and sloppy.
They fail to make the organization's goals clear.
Their managers and workers both lack direction.
This shows in their lack of organization.
These organizations are chaotic.

Some organizations' leaders fail to predict the future.
They don't see the major trends in the industry.
They are overmatched by their competitors.
They make poor decisions.
These organizations will shrink.

³¹You must know all about these six weaknesses.
You must understand the philosophies that lead to defeat.
When a general arrives, you can know what he will do.
You must study each general carefully.

You must control your field position. 3
It will always strengthen your army.

³You must predict the enemy to overpower him and win.
You must analyze the obstacles, dangers, and distances.
This is the best way to command.

⁶Understand your field position before you go to battle.
Then you will win.
You can fail to understand your field position and still fight.
Then you will lose.

¹⁰You must provoke battle when you will certainly win.
It doesn't matter what you are ordered.
The government may order you not to fight.
Despite that, you must always fight when you will win.

¹⁴Sometimes provoking a battle will lead to a loss.
The government may order you to fight.
Despite that, you must avoid battle when you will lose.

Recognize these six weaknesses in any organization.
Choosing to stay with the wrong organization leads to failure.
If you take a job in a weak organization, you know what will happen.
You must weigh each potential employer carefully.

3 You must choose your job situation.
Your control creates success in your career.

You must foresee how to pick the right employer.
You must analyze difficulties, problems, and needs.
This is the best way to build a career.

You must understand these issues when you look for a job.
If you do, you will succeed.
If you fail to find the right position, you can still get a job.
However, you will not be successful.

You must go after a job that will make you successful.
Forget your other priorities.
You may find it difficult to go after this job.
Still, you must go after it when the opportunity is real.

Sometimes, winning a promotion will hurt your career.
Your employer may give you the promotion.
Still, if you accept it, you will fail.

[17]You must advance without desiring praise.
You must retreat without fearing shame.
The only correct move is to preserve your troops.
This is how you serve your country.
This is how you reward your nation.

Think of your soldiers as little children. 4
You can make them follow you into a deep river.
Treat them as your beloved children.
You can lead them all to their deaths.

[5]Some leaders are generous but cannot use their men.
They love their men but cannot command them.
Their men are unruly and disorganized.
These leaders create spoiled children.
Their soldiers are useless.

You may know what your soldiers will do in an attack. 5
You may not know if the enemy is vulnerable to attack.
You will then win only half the time.
You may know that the enemy is vulnerable to attack.
You may not know if your men have the capability of
attacking him.
You will still win only half the time.
You may know that the enemy is vulnerable to attack.
You may know that your men are ready to attack.
You may not, however, know how to position yourself in the
field for battle.
You will still win only half the time.

You must never take a job for the sake of pride.
Abandon a good job without embarrassment.
Your only goal is to advance your career.
This is how you serve your family.
This is how you ensure your success.

4 Think of your job experiences as stepping stones.
They will support you in an uncertain future.
Pick jobs with care and understanding.
They will serve you faithfully.

Some care only about their salary, not where their jobs lead.
They can love their work, but it leads nowhere.
Their job experience is spotty and unfocused.
These people spoil their future.
Their experience is useless.

5 You can know that your experience appeals to employers.
Nevertheless, you must know how to win jobs against rivals.
If you don't, you have done only part of your job.
You can know how to beat rivals.
Nevertheless, you must also know that your experience will appeal
to employers.
If you don't, you have done only part of your job.
You can know how to beat rivals.
You can know how to appeal to employers.
Nevertheless, you must also know exactly how to choose the right
job situation.
If you don't, you have done only part of your job.

[11]You must know how to make war.
You can then act without confusion.
You can attempt anything.

[14]We say:
Know the enemy and know yourself.
Your victory will be painless.
Know the weather and the field.
Your victory will be complete.

♦ ♦ ♦

You must know how to select a job.
You can then act with certainty.
You can go as far as you want.

We say this:
Know your rivals and your abilities.
Then success is easy.
Understand opportunities and organizations.
Then your success is assured.

♦ ♦ ♦

Related Articles from *Sun Tzu's Playbook*

In chapter ten, Sun Tzu discusses the use of temporary positions in building relation-ships with voters. To learn the step-by-step techniques involved, we recommend the Sun Tzu's Art of War Playbook articles listed below.

4.6.1 Spread-Out Conditions: recognizing opportunities that are too large.

4.6.2 Constricted Conditions: identifying and using constricted positions.

4.6.3 Barricaded Conditions: the issues related to the extremes of obstacles.

4.6.4 Wide-Open Conditions: the issues related to an absence of barriers.

4.6.5 Fixed Conditions: positions with extreme holding power.

4.6.6 Sensitive Conditions: positions with no holding power on pursuing opportunities.

4.7 Competitive Weakness: how certain opportunities can bring out our weaknesses.

4.7.1 Command Weaknesses: the character flaws of leaders and how to exploit them.

4.7.2 Group Weaknesses: organizational weakness and where groups fail.

4.8 Climate Support: choosing new positions based on future changes.

4.9 Opportunity Mapping: two-dimensional tool for comparing opportunity probabilities.

Scattering

Easy.

Open

Intersecting

Dangerous   Confused

Red

Deadly

Chapter 11

九地

Types of Terrain (Career Stages)

This chapter describes nine different situations that tend to evolve as an army penetrates ever more deeply into enemy territory. Each of these situations or stages of development has a clear tactical focus. In examining your professional growth, these stages provide a useful framework for evaluating the nature of your current position.

The chapter's first section describes the nine campaign stages and the specific tactical focuses that they demand.

Sun Tzu then describes how to keep opponents from organizing and how to defend against invasion.

The third section discusses the general management of an invasion into enemy territory.

Sun Tzu then addresses how to prepare the right response to attack beforehand and how to use adversity to unite your forces.

He then discusses the functions of a leader.

In the sixth section, Sun Tzu reviews the stages of a campaign, with an emphasis on troop psychology.

Sun Tzu then emphasizes knowledge and unity as the keys to a successful campaign, with a special emphasis on the ability to recover from initial setbacks.

The final section addresses the need to set the proper tone for a campaign at the very start.

Types of Terrain

Use the art of war. 1
Know when the terrain will scatter you.
Know when the terrain will be easy.
Know when the terrain will be disputed.
Know when the terrain is open.
Know when the terrain is intersecting.
Know when the terrain is dangerous.
Know when the terrain is bad.
Know when the terrain is confined.
Know when the terrain is deadly.

[11]Warring parties must sometimes fight inside their own
territory.
This is scattering terrain.

[13]When you enter hostile territory, your penetration is shallow.
This is easy terrain.

[15]Some terrain gives you an advantageous position.
But it gives others an advantageous position as well.
This will be disputed terrain.

Career Stages

1 Build your career wisely.
Know when your position is tenuous.
Know when your position is easy.
Know when your position is contentious.
Know when your position is open.
Know when your position is shared.
Know when your position is serious.
Know when your position is bad.
Know when your position is limited.
Know when your position is do-or-die.

You must sometimes defend your responsibilities against a new rival.
This is a tenuous position.

When you move into a new position, your ideas are new.
This is an easy position.

Your next possible position could be very rewarding.
Nevertheless, rivals can win this position as well.
This is a contentious position.

[18]You can use some terrain to advance easily.
Others can advance along with you.
This is open terrain.

[21]Everyone shares access to a given area.
The first one to arrive there can gather a larger group than
anyone else.
This is intersecting terrain.

[24]You can penetrate deeply into hostile territory.
Then many hostile cities are behind you.
This is dangerous terrain.

[27]There are mountain forests.
There are dangerous obstructions.
There are reservoirs.
Everyone confronts these obstacles on a campaign.
They make bad terrain.

[32]In some areas, the entry passage is narrow.
You are closed in as you try to get out of them.
In this type of area, a few people can effectively attack your
much larger force.
This is confined terrain.

[36]You can sometimes survive only if you fight quickly.
You will die if you delay.
This is deadly terrain.

You make easy progress in your job.
Rivals, however, can still come in at any time.
This is an open position.

Several people share the same responsibilities.
If you can develop good working partnerships, you will be
successful.
This is a shared position.

You have been successful in your job.
You have left many rivals in the organization behind you.
This is a serious position.

Your professional future is difficult and unknown.
Your job advancement is slow.
Your internal support is uncertain.
All people have such difficulties at some time in their working life.
This is a bad position.

In some careers, there is a key transition point.
You rely on a few key relationships to get through it.
Your entire career can be undone if rivals know how dependent you
are.
This is a limited position.

Sometimes you succeed only if you take a chance.
You will fail if you delay.
This is a do-or-die job position.

[39]To be successful, you must control scattering terrain by avoiding battle.

Control easy terrain by not stopping.

Control disputed terrain by not attacking.

Control open terrain by staying with the enemy's forces.

Control intersecting terrain by uniting with your allies.

Control dangerous terrain by plundering.

Control bad terrain by keeping on the move.

Control confined terrain by using surprise.

Control deadly terrain by fighting.

Go to an area that is known to be good for waging war. **2**
Use it to cut off the enemy's contact between his front and back lines.

Prevent his small parties from relying on his larger force.

Stop his strong divisions from rescuing his weak ones.

Prevent his officers from getting their men together.

Chase his soldiers apart to stop them from amassing.

Harass them to prevent their ranks from forming.

[8]When joining battle gives you an advantage, you must do it.

When it isn't to your benefit, you must avoid it.

[10]A daring soldier may ask:

"A large, organized enemy army and its general are coming.

What do I do to prepare for them?"

To be successful, avoid tenuous positions by not leaving openings for rivals.

In easy positions, don't stop making progress.

In contentious positions, avoid competing for jobs.

In open positions, keep up with your rivals.

In shared positions, make good alliances.

In serious positions, concentrate on generating results.

In bad positions, keep yourself productive.

In limited positions, be inventive.

In do-or-die positions, fight to make yourself successful.

2. Find a position that makes you successful.

You can use your position to cut off organizational support for your opponents.

Prevent small opposing groups from joining together.

Stop rivals from finding support from management.

Prevent rival managers from aligning people against you.

Stop any opposition from banding together.

Pressure opponents to stop them from getting organized.

When opposing others creates an opportunity, fight them.

When it doesn't create an opportunity, avoid fighting them.

You may ask:

"A senior, powerful opponent is plotting against me.
 What should I do?"

¹³Tell him:
"First seize an area that the enemy must have.
Then he will pay attention to you.
Mastering speed is the essence of war.
Take advantage of a large enemy's inability to keep up.
Use a philosophy of avoiding difficult situations.
Attack the area where he doesn't expect you."

You must use the philosophy of an invader. 3
Invade deeply and then concentrate your forces.
This controls your men without oppressing them.

⁴Get your supplies from the riches of the territory.
It is sufficient to supply your whole army.

⁶Take care of your men and do not overtax them.
Your esprit de corps increases your momentum.
Keep your army moving and plan for surprises.
Make it difficult for the enemy to count your forces.
Position your men where there is no place to run.
They will then face death without fleeing.
They will find a way to survive.
Your officers and men will fight to their utmost.

¹⁴Military officers who are committed lose their fear.
When they have nowhere to run, they must stand firm.
Deep in enemy territory, they are captives.
Since they cannot escape, they will fight.

There is an answer.

You must move to a place where he cannot touch you.

He may want to damage your career.

The freedom to move is the essence of building your career.

Use the inability of a serious opponent to follow you.

Your goal should be to avoid difficult positions.

Move to another position when opponents are unprepared.

3 You must have the goal of making yourself an expert.

Get deeply involved in your job and focus on it.

This channels your skills without stifling them.

Use the value of your expertise to generate income.

Your expertise must be capable of supporting your goals.

Hone your skills and don't get stretched too thin.

Use teamwork to increase your momentum.

Keep your career moving forward and plan for surprises.

Make it difficult for rivals to know who supports you.

Focus your efforts and don't let yourself be distracted.

Face all crises without losing your focus.

You will find a way to succeed.

Your skills and abilities will serve you well.

If you are committed to success, you lose the fear of failure.

If you are focused on your job, you can stand firm.

When you are committed, your skills are productive.

Since your expertise is needed, you will succeed.

[18]Commit your men completely.
Without being posted, they will be on guard.
Without being asked, they will get what is needed.
Without being forced, they will be dedicated.
Without being given orders, they can be trusted.

[23]Stop them from guessing by removing all their doubts.
Stop them from dying by giving them no place to run.

[25]Your officers may not be rich.
Nevertheless, they still desire plunder.
They may die young.
Nevertheless, they still want to live forever.

[29]You must order the time of attack.
Officers and men may sit and weep until their lapels are wet.
When they stand up, tears may stream down their cheeks.
Put them in a position where they cannot run.
They will show the greatest courage under fire.

Make good use of war. 4
This demands instant reflexes.
You must develop these instant reflexes.
Act like an ordinary mountain snake.
If people strike your head then stop them with your tail.
If they strike your tail then stop them with your head.
If they strike your middle then use both your head and tail.

Commit yourself completely to your organization.
Without being told, you must see what needs to be done.
Without being asked, you must do what is needed.
Without being pressured, you must be dedicated.
Without being watched, you must be trustworthy.

Stop any second-guessing by making commitments clear.
Avoid failure by leaving yourself no excuses.

You may not be rich.
Nevertheless, you still want wealth.
You may fail.
It shouldn't be because you didn't commit to success.

You must be in control when you leave a position.
You may leave even when your employer begs you to stay.
While in the position, you must be committed to your organization.
You should never switch jobs to avoid a problem.
You must be courageous in your career.

4 Make good use of job evaluations.
Evaluations demand instant responses.
You must practice these responses beforehand.
You should be quick to react.
If interviewers attack your skills, respond with your experience.
If interviewers attack your experience, highlight your expertise.
If they see you as average, emphasize your experience and skills.

[8]A daring soldier asks:
"Can any army imitate these instant reflexes?"
We answer:
"It can."

[12]To command and get the most out of proud people, you
must study adversity.
People work together when they are in the same boat during
a storm.
In this situation, one rescues the other just as the right
hand helps the left.

[15]Use adversity correctly.
Tether your horses and bury your wagon's wheels.
Still, you can't depend on this alone.
An organized force is braver than lone individuals.
This is the art of organization.
Put the tough and weak together.
You must also use the terrain.

[22]Make good use of war.
Unite your men as one.
Never let them give up.

The commander must be a military professional. 5
This requires confidence and detachment.
You must maintain dignity and order.
You must control what your men see and hear.
They must follow you without knowing your plans.

You may question this.

Should you prepare all your responses?

There is only one answer.

You must!

To get the most out of an evaluation, you must respond well under pressure.

Remember that you and your evaluator both have a problem to solve.

You can help each other when you both realize that you are partners in evaluating your work.

Respond well under pressure.

Show your desire to dedicate yourself to the organization.

Even this isn't enough.

Try to become a partner with your supervisor.

This is the art of collaborating.

You can solve his problems.

You must understand his problems.

Make good use of a job evaluation.

Put all your skills into a simple package.

Show that you are determined.

5 You must be a professional.
This requires confidence and detachment.

You must maintain your dignity and control.

You must control what a potential employer sees and hears.

Employers must believe you without knowing your plans.

⁶You can reinvent your men's roles.

You can change your plans.

You can use your men without their understanding.

⁹You must shift your campgrounds.

You must take detours from the ordinary routes.

You must use your men without giving them your strategy.

¹²A commander provides what is needed now.

This is like climbing high and being willing to kick away your ladder.

You must be able to lead your men deeply into different surrounding territory.

And yet, you can discover the opportunity to win.

¹⁶You must drive men like a flock of sheep.

You must drive them to march.

You must drive them to attack.

You must never let them know where you are headed.

You must unite them into a great army.

You must then drive them against all opposition.

This is the job of a true commander.

²³You must adapt to the different terrain.

You must adapt to find an advantage.

You must manage your people's affections.

You must study all these skills.

You can use your experience in different ways.

You can change your goals.

You can reshape your career without planning.

You must change employers.

You must create your own promotion path.

You can use your expertise without giving your plans away.

You must provide what employers need at the moment.

You must be willing to go out on a limb and take a risk to be successful.

You must get deeply involved with your employer's business to discover difficulties.

These difficulties create the opportunities that you need to succeed.

You must motivate supervisors to allow you to work.

You must inspire them to change.

You must entice them to act.

You must never let them take you for granted.

You must bring the people you work with together.

You must unite them to overcome problems.

This is the hallmark of a successful career.

You must adapt to every stage in your career.

You must adjust to your situation to create opportunities.

You must know how to use people's emotions.

You must learn all these skills.

Always use the philosophy of invasion. 6
Deep invasions concentrate your forces.
Shallow invasions scatter your forces.
When you leave your country and cross the border, you must
take control.
This is always critical ground.
You can sometimes move in any direction.
This is always intersecting ground.
You can penetrate deeply into a territory.
This is always dangerous ground.
You penetrate only a little way.
This is always easy ground.
Your retreat is closed and the path ahead tight.
This is always confined ground.
There is sometimes no place to run.
This is always deadly ground.

[16]To use scattering terrain correctly, you must inspire your
men's devotion.
On easy terrain, you must keep in close communication.
On disputed terrain, you try to hamper the enemy's progress.
On open terrain, you must carefully defend your chosen position.
On intersecting terrain, you must solidify your alliances.
On dangerous terrain, you must ensure your food supplies.
On bad terrain, you must keep advancing along the road.
On confined terrain, you must stop information leaks from
your headquarters.
On deadly terrain, you must show what you can do by
killing the enemy.

6 Your career must be that of a specialist.
Commitment to your specialty focuses your efforts.
Weak commitments dissipate your skills.
At the beginning of a commitment to a profession, you must be disciplined.
This is a critical time.
Your interests join with those of others.
You must create good partnerships.
You can dedicate yourself totally to your employer.
This is always a serious stage.
All jobs look promising when you first start them.
This is always the easy stage of a job.
Your contacts are so limited that you rely on a few people.
This is the limited stage of a career.
A career can narrow to one big decision.
This is the risky stage.

To succeed in a tenuous position, you must show your devotion to your job.
In an easy position, you must communicate with employers.
In a contentious position, you must create obstacles for your rivals.
In an open position, you must defend your position against your rivals.
In a shared position, you must join your partners.
In a serious position, you must generate value.
In a bad position, you must find another employer.
In a limited position, you must defend your position with top people.
In a do-or-die position, you must prove yourself by succcessfully meeting the challenge.

²⁵Make your men feel like an army.
Surround them and they will defend themselves.
If they cannot avoid it, they will fight.
If they are under pressure, they will obey.

Do the right thing when you don't know your 7
different enemies' plans.
Don't attempt to meet them.

³You don't know the position of mountain forests, dangerous
obstructions, and reservoirs?
Then you cannot march the army.
You don't have local guides?
You won't get any of the benefits of the terrain.

⁷There are many factors in war.
You may lack knowledge of any one of them.
If so, it is wrong to take a nation into war.

¹⁰You must be able to control your government's war.
If you divide a big nation, it will be unable to put together a
large force.
Increase your enemy's fear of your ability.
Prevent his forces from getting together and organizing.

Make your job experience valuable.
If your abilities are stretched, they will develop.
When you refuse to quit, you will work hard.
When you are under pressure, you will succeed.

7 Do the right thing when you don't understand an employer's thinking:
Don't try to meet with him.

You don't understand an employer's goals, problems, and difficulties?
Then you should not move into or up in that organization.
You don't have people to help you within the organization?
You won't find opportunities there.

There is so much to know in building a career.
You must analyze every opportunity.
Otherwise, it is wrong to seek advancement.

You must be able to influence your supervisor's success.
A large organization has to consider the needs of a great number of people.
Increase your rivals' fear of your influence.
Prevent them from getting together to oppose you.

¹⁴Do the right thing and do not arrange outside alliances
before their time.
You will not have to assert your authority prematurely.
Trust only yourself and your self-interest.
This increases the enemy's fear of you.
You can make one of his allies withdraw.
His whole nation can fall.

²⁰Distribute rewards without worrying about having a system.
Halt without the government's command.
Attack with the whole strength of your army.
Use your army as if it were a single man.

²⁴Attack with skill.
Do not discuss it.
Attack when you have an advantage.
Do not talk about the dangers.
When you can launch your army into deadly ground, even if
it stumbles, it can still survive.
You can be weakened in a deadly battle and yet be stronger
afterward.

³⁰Even a large force can fall into misfortune.
If you fall behind, however, you can still turn defeat into victory.
You must use the skills of war.
To survive, you must adapt yourself to your enemy's purpose.
You must stay with him no matter where he goes.
It may take a thousand miles to kill the general.
If you correctly understand him, you can find the skill to do it.

Act correctly and don't depend upon politics within the
organization.
Then you won't have to lobby for promotions.
Trust yourself and your own resources.
This decreases any rival's source of information.
You may convince your rival's supporters to abandon him.
His whole campaign may then collapse.

Give everyone credit for any success you have.
Stop what is unnecessary without being told.
Work to your utmost every day.
Use all your skills together.

Go after new positions with skill.
Don't let anyone know.
Be aggressive when you discover an opportunity.
Don't worry about the risks.
You may lose when you try for a new position, but you can still keep
your current position.
You may be discouraged by losing, but you are more likely to win a
promotion afterward.

You can win many promotions and still run into problems.
If you fail to get a promotion, you can turn rejection into success.
You must use your skills to build your career.
To succeed, you must adapt to your organization's needs.
You must stay in sync with your organization.
It can take years and years to rise to the top.
If you understand your organization, you have the skill to succeed.

Manage your government correctly at the start of a war. 8
Close your borders and tear up passports.
Block the passage of envoys.
Encourage politicians at headquarters to stay out of it.
You must use any means to put an end to politics.
Your enemy's people will leave you an opening.
You must instantly invade through it.

8Immediately seize a place that they love.
Do it quickly.
Trample any border to pursue the enemy.
Use your judgment about when to fight.

12Doing the right thing at the start of war is like
approaching a woman.
Your enemy's men must open the door.
After that, you should act like a streaking rabbit.
The enemy will be unable to catch you.

✦ ✦ ✦

8 Do the right things when you first accept a new job.
Protect your responsibilities and keep rivals out.
Don't communicate indirectly.
Give managers the confidence to let you do your job.
You must use any means to avoid internal politics.
Eventually the organization will have a better job opening.
You must instantly pursue it.

Quickly win your superiors' confidence.
Waste no time.
Go beyond your duties to solve problems.
Use your best judgment about when to stand out.

Success when you start a new job requires winning people over to
your side.
You will eventually have an opportunity to move up.
When it happens, you should act quickly.
Your rivals will be unable to catch up with you.

✦ ✦ ✦

Related Articles from *Sun Tzu's Playbook*

In chapter eleven, Sun Tzu explains instant situation response. To learn the step-by-step techniques involved, we recommend the Sun Tzu's Art of War Playbook *articles listed below.*

6.0 Situation Response: selecting the actions most appropriate to a situation.

6.1 Situation Recognition: situation recognition in making advances.

6.1.1 Conditioned Reflexes: how we develop automatic, instantaneous responses.

6.1.2 Prioritizing Conditions: parsing complex competitive conditions into simple responses.

6.2 Campaign Evaluation: how we justify continued investment in an ongoing campaign.

6.2.1 Campaign Flow: seeing campaigns as a series of situations that flow logically from one to another.

6.2.2 Campaign Goals: assessing the value of a campaign by a larger mission.

6.3 Campaign Patterns: how knowing campaign stages gives us insight into our situation.

6.3.1 Early-Stage Situations: the common situations that arise the earliest in campaigns.

6.3.2 Middle-Stage Situations: how progress creates transitional situations in campaigns.

6.3.3 Late-Stage Situations: understanding the final and most dangerous stages of campaigns.

6.4 Nine Situations: the nine common competitive situations.

6.4.1 Dissipating Situations: situations where defensive unity is destroyed.

6.4.2 Easy Situations: recognizing situations of easy initial progress.

6.4.3 Contentious Situations: identifying situations that invite conflict.

6.4.4 Open Situations: recognizing situations that are races without a course.

6.4.5 Intersecting Situations: recognizing situations that bring people together.

6.4.6 Serious Situations: identifying situations where resources can be cut off.

6.4.7 Difficult Situations: recognizing situations where serious barriers must be overcome.

6.4.8 Limited Situations: identifying situations defined by a bottleneck.

6.4.9 Desperate Situations: identifying situations where destruction is possible.

6.5 Nine Responses: using the best responses to the nine common competitive situations.

6.5.1 Dissipating Response: responding to dissipation by the use of offense as defense.

6.5.2 Easy Response: responding to easy situations by overcoming complacency.

6.5.3 Contentious Response: responding to contentious situations by knowing how to avoid conflict.

6.5.4 Open Response: responding to open situations by keeping up with the opposition.

6.5.5 Intersecting Response: the formation of situational alliances.

6.5.6 Serious Response: responding to serious situations by finding immediate income.

6.5.7 Difficult Response: the role of persistence in responding to difficult situations.

6.5.8 Limited Response: the need for secret speed in limited situations.

6.5.9 Desperate Response: using all our resources in responding to desperate situations.

6.6 Campaign Pause: knowing when to stop advancing a position.

Chapter 12

火攻

Attacking with Fire (Winning a Job)

Although Sun Tzu uses this chapter to cover a specific weapon, fire, its broader subject is using any weapon, with an emphasis on leveraging forces in the environment as weapons. For you as a job seeker, these lessons map out the best way to leverage your current work environment to win a new job.

Sun Tzu begins by describing the five specific targets for environmental attack. He also addresses the critical importance of timing in these attacks.

Then he emphasizes that the attack itself is less important than the response to it. An attack does not create an opportunity. It is the response to it that creates the opportunity.

Sun Tzu then briefly compares using fire and water as environmental weapons.

He ends the discussion with the need to control emotional responses in both undertaking and responding to attacks.

Attacking with Fire

SUN TZU SAID:

There are five ways of attacking with fire. 1
The first is burning troops.
The second is burning supplies.
The third is burning supply transport.
The fourth is burning storehouses.
The fifth is burning camps.

7To make fire, you must have the resources.
To build a fire, you must prepare the raw materials.

9To attack with fire, you must be in the right season.
To start a fire, you must have the time.

11Choose the right season.
The weather must be dry.

13Choose the right time.
Pick a season when the grass is as high as the side of a cart.

15You can tell the proper days by the stars in the night sky.
You want days when the wind rises in the morning.

Winning a Job

1 There are five targets for winning a job.
The first is a person.
The second is a position.
The third is an area of expertise.
The fourth is an organization.
The fifth is an industry.

To go after a job, you must have the right qualifications.
To win a job, you must package your experience.

To win a job, you must go after it at the right time.
To look for a job, you must invest your time.

Choose the right time.
Potential employers must need people.

Be careful of your timing.
Pick a time when an employer can hire.

To know the right time, learn about a job before others do.
You want to pick a time when the need to hire is building.

Everyone attacks with fire. 2
You must create five different situations with fire and be able
to adjust to them.

3You start a fire inside the enemy's camp.
Then attack the enemy's periphery.

5You launch a fire attack, but the enemy remains calm.
Wait and do not attack.

7The fire reaches its height.
Follow its path if you can.
If you can't follow it, stay where you are.

10Spreading fires on the outside of camp can kill.
You can't always get fire inside the enemy's camp.
Take your time in spreading it.

13Set the fire when the wind is at your back.
Don't attack into the wind.
Daytime winds last a long time.
Night winds fade quickly.

17Every army must know how to adjust to the five possible
attacks by fire.
Use many men to guard against them.

2 Everyone tries to win jobs these ways.
You must be able to recognize five different hiring situations and respond to them.

You hear about a new job within a target organization.
You make contact from the outside to find out about it.

You contact someone about a job, but there is no response.
Wait and do not appear desperate.

Wait until the organization has a formal hiring process.
Follow that process if you can.
If the process works against you, stay where you are.

Sometimes advertising your availability can help find a job.
You don't have to know of a specific opening.
Take your time putting out the word.

Look for a new job when you have had a great success.
Don't look when you have had problems.
Well-publicized successes serve you a long time.
Less visible successes are forgotten quickly.

You must master all five of these different approaches to winning a new job.
You must be constantly prepared to use them.

When you use fire to assist your attacks, you are clever. 3
Water can add force to an attack.
You can also use water to disrupt an enemy.
It does not, however, take his resources.

You win in battle by getting the opportunity to attack. 4
It is dangerous if you fail to study how to accomplish this
achievement.
As commander, you cannot waste your opportunities.

4We say:
A wise leader plans success.
A good general studies it.
If there is little to be gained, don't act.
If there is little to win, do not use your men.
If there is no danger, don't fight.

10As leader, you cannot let your anger interfere with the
success of your forces.
As commander, you cannot let yourself become enraged
before you go to battle.
Join the battle only when it is in your advantage to act.
If there is no advantage in joining a battle, stay put.

14Anger can change back into happiness.
Rage can change back into joy.
A nation once destroyed cannot be brought back to life.
Dead men do not return to the living.

3 When you go after jobs to advance your career, you are being smart.
Getting pay raises improves your standard of living.
You can use pay raises to stand out from rivals.
Pay raises alone, however, doesn't win a position away from a rival.

4 You win jobs by discovering opportunities in the market.
It is a mistake not to concentrate your efforts on discovering opportunities.
In building a career, you cannot waste any opportunity.

We say this:
A smart person plans his career.
A successful person studies the job market.
If a new job doesn't advance your career, don't go after it.
If it doesn't open doors, don't waste your efforts.
If your current position is still valuable, don't move.

You must never let your emotions affect your decision to change jobs.
You must never go after a new job simply because you are upset with your current one.
Make a job change only when it is to your advantage.
If there is no advantage in moving, stay put.

Emotions change with time.
Unhappiness in your job can turn back to pleasure.
An organization badly abandoned cannot be rejoined.
A job you leave in anger cannot be restored.

[18]This fact must make a wise leader cautious.
A good general is on guard.

[20]Your philosophy must be to keep the nation peaceful and
the army intact.

✦ ✦ ✦

Knowing this, you must be careful.
A bright person is always watching.

Your goal must be to avoid conflict within your organization and to keep your career moving forward.

◆ ◆ ◆

Related Articles from *Sun Tzu's Playbook*

In chapter twelve, Sun Tzu discusses the use of environmental weapons. To learn the step-by-step techniques involved, we recommend the Sun Tzu's Art of War Playbook *articles listed below.*

9.0 Understanding Vulnerability: the use of common environmental attacks.

9.1 Climate Vulnerability: our vulnerability to environmental crises arising from change.

9.1.1 Climate Rivals: how changing conditions create opponents.

9.1.2 Threat Development: how changing conditions create environmental threats.

9.2 Points of Vulnerability: our points of vulnerability during an environmental crisis.

9.2.1 Personnel Risk: the vulnerability of key individuals.

9.2.2 Immediate Resource Risk: the vulnerability of the resources required for immediate use.

9.2.3 Transportation/Communication Risk: how firestorms choke normal channels of movement and communication.

9.2.4 Asset Risk: the threats to our fixed assets.

9.2.5 Organizational Risk: targeting the roles and responsibilities within an organization.

9.3 Crisis Leadership: maintaining the support of our supporters during attacks.

9.3.1 Mutual Danger: how we use mutual danger to create mutual strength.

9.3.2 Message Control: communication methods to use during a crisis.

9.4 Crisis Defense: how vulnerabilities are exploited and defended during a crisis.

9.4.1 Division Defense: preventing organizational division during a crisis.

9.4.2 Panic Defense: preventing the mistakes arising from panic during a crisis.

9.4.3 Defending Openings: how to defend openings created by a crisis.

9.4.4 Defending Alliances: dealing with guilt by association.

9.4.5 Defensive Balance: using short-term conditions to tip the balance in a crisis.

9.5 Crisis Exploitation: how to successfully use an opponent's crisis.

9.5.1 Adversarial Opportunities: how our opponents' crises can create opportunities.

9.5.2 Avoiding Emotion: the danger of exploiting environmental vulnerabilities for purely emotion reasons.

9.6 Constant Vigilance: where to focus our attention to preserve our positions.

Chapter 13

用 間

Using Spies (Using Contacts)

In his final chapter, Sun Tzu addresses what he considers to be
the most important element of strategy: information. A number
of earlier chapters address the importance of information in their
closing sections; here, in the closing chapter, Sun Tzu returns
to that topic with a special emphasis on developing sources of
information. For anyone concerned about his or her career, Sun
Tzu's lessons about spies apply directly to creating an invaluable
network of personal contacts in the job market.

Sun Tzu begins by describing the many costs of war which can
be minimized by the right information. He makes the point that
this information must come from people as sources.

Sun Tzu then lists the five different types of information and
information sources.

He then discusses techniques for evaluating information and
managing information sources.

Then he makes the point that before you tackle a specific
problem you must first find sources that provide a complete picture
of that problem.

The closing section points out that the history of competition
shows that success depends first on the cultivation of good
information sources.

Using Spies

SUN TZU SAID:

All successful armies require thousands of men. 1
They invade and march thousands of miles.
Whole families are destroyed.
Other families must be heavily taxed.
Every day, a large amount of money must be spent.

6Internal and external events force people to move.
They are unable to work while on the road.
They are unable to find and hold a useful job.
This affects seventy percent of thousands of families.

10You can watch and guard for years.
Then a single battle can determine victory in a day.
Despite this, bureaucrats worship the value of their salary
money too dearly.
They remain ignorant of the enemy's condition.
The result is cruel.

15They are not leaders of men.
They are not servants of the state.
They are not masters of victory.

Using Contacts

1 Building a career involves thousands of people.
It requires traveling thousands of miles.
It can destroy your family.
It will financially strain your family.
Every day, building your career is costly.

Internal and external events force people to change jobs.
People are dislocated and unable to work.
They are unable to find and hold useful jobs.
This affects their families.

You can work at your profession for years.
A single contact can determine your success in a day.
Despite all this, many people think that the value of their job is its salary.
They remain ignorant of what their position makes possible.
The result is devastating.

These people are not truly successful.
They do not truly support their families.
They are not masters of their future.

¹⁸You need a creative leader and a worthy commander.
You must move your troops to the right places to beat others.
You must accomplish your attack and escape unharmed.
This requires foreknowledge.
You can obtain foreknowledge.
You can't get it from demons or spirits.
You can't see it from professional experience.
You can't check it with analysis.
You can only get it from other people.
You must always know the enemy's situation.

You must use five types of spies. 2
You need local spies.
You need inside spies.
You need double agents.
You need doomed spies.
You need surviving spies.

⁷You need all five types of spies.
No one must discover your methods.
You will then be able to put together a true picture.
This is the commander's most valuable resource.

¹¹You need local spies.
Get them by hiring people from the countryside.

¹³You need inside spies.
Win them by subverting government officials.

You must be a creative worker and a valuable manager.
You must pursue your career in the right places to succeed.
You must surpass others and know when to move on.
This requires information.
You can get this advance information.
You won't get it from astrology.
You won't get it from past experience.
You can't reason this information out.
You can only get it by asking people questions.
You must always know your job environment.

2 You must use five types of personal contacts.
You need contacts among your organization's customers.
You need contacts in your organization.
You need contacts in competing organizations.
You need contacts in the employment industry.
You need contacts in your industry's news organizations.

You must use all five types of contacts.
No one must know everything you do.
You can put together a true picture of your situation.
Information is your most valuable resource.

You need information about your organization.
Get it by winning friends among customers and clients.

You need information from within your organization.
You get it by making friends of managers and assistants.

¹⁵You need double agents.
Discover enemy agents and convert them.

¹⁷You need doomed spies.
Deceive professionals into being captured.
Let them know your orders.
They then take those orders to your enemy.

²¹You need surviving spies.
Someone must return with a report.

Your job is to build a complete army. 3
No relations are as intimate as the ones with spies.
No rewards are too generous for spies.
No work is as secret as that of spies.

⁵If you aren't clever and wise, you can't use spies.
If you aren't fair and just, you can't use spies.
If you can't see the small subtleties, you won't get the truth
from spies.

⁸Pay attention to small, trifling details!
Spies are helpful in every area.

¹⁰Spies are the first to hear information, so they must not
spread information.
Spies who give your location or talk to others must be killed
along with those to whom they have talked.

You need information about similar organizations.
You get it by making friends in competing organizations.

You need contacts in the employment industry.
Let them know you might be looking for a new position.
Let them know your interests.
They will take that information to competing organizations.

You need contacts in your industry's news organizations.
You must know the latest developments in the job market.

3 Your job is to develop a complete career.
No friendships are as important as those with your contacts.
No reward is too generous for good information.
No knowledge is as confidential as that obtained from your friends.

You must be bright and perceptive to develop a network.
You must be open and unbiased to develop friendships.
If you aren't sensitive to subtleties, you won't find the truth in what
people tell you.

You must pay close attention to small details.
Contacts are helpful in every area.

Your contacts must keep the confidential information that you give
them a secret.
You must cut off relationships with those who are likely to spread
the wrong information about you.

You may want to attack an army's position. 4
You may want to attack a certain fortification.
You may want to kill people in a certain place.
You must first know the guarding general.
You must know his left and right flanks.
You must know his hierarchy.
You must know the way in.
You must know where different people are stationed.
You must demand this information from your spies.

[10]You want to know the enemy spies in order to convert
them into your men.
You find a source of information and bribe them.
You must bring them in with you.
You must obtain them as double agents and use them as
your emissaries.

[14]Do this correctly and carefully.
You can contact both local and inside spies and obtain their
support.
Do this correctly and carefully.
You create doomed spies by deceiving professionals.
You can use them to give false information.
Do this correctly and carefully.
You must have surviving spies capable of bringing you
information at the right time.

4 You may want to move to another organization.
You may be interested in a certain type of work.
You may want to win a specific job.
You must first know the target organization's manager.
You must know the structure of his organization.
You must know who makes the decisions.
You must know what the organization needs.
You must know who the key people are.
You must get this information from your contacts.

You want to know people in other organizations in order to win
them over.
You must be willing to spend time entertaining them.
You must stay on good terms with them.
You must get them on your side and have them further your
reputation.

You must do this carefully.
You need to make friends and supporters throughout your own
organization.
You must also do this selectively.
You can involve employment agencies without hiring them.
You don't have to be completely honest with them.
You must do this quietly as well.
You need friends who get the latest news in your industry and then
contact you about it.

[21]These are the five different types of intelligence work.
You must be certain to master them all.
You must be certain to create double agents.
You cannot afford to be too cost conscious in creating these double agents.

This technique created the success of ancient Shang. 5
This is how the Shang held its dynasty.

[3]You must always be careful of your success.
Learn from Lu Ya of Shang.

[5]Be a smart commander and a good general.
You do this by using your best and brightest people for spying.
This is how you achieve the greatest success.
This is how you meet the necessities of war.
The whole army's position and ability to move depends on these spies.

There are five different types of relationships.
You must be certain to master them all.
You must have friends outside your organization.
You cannot invest too much time in developing contacts outside your organization.

5 This is how people have been successful in their careers. This is how they have risen in their industries.

You must build your career with care.
Learn from the history of past success.

You must be a good manager and a good friend.
You must know the best and brightest people as your contacts.
This is how you achieve the greatest success.
This is how you satisfy your need for advancement.
Your current job and your ability to change positions depend on your contacts.

♦ ♦ ♦

♦ ♦ ♦

Related Articles from *Sun Tzu's Playbook*

In his final chapter, Sun Tzu explains how to use information channels. To learn the step-by-step techniques involved, we recommend the Sun Tzu's Art of War Playbook *articles listed below.*

2.0.0 Developing Perspective: adding depth to competitive analysis.

2.1 Information Value: knowledge and communication as the basis of strategy.

2.1.1 Information Limits: making good decisions with limited information.

2.1.3 Strategic Deception: misinformation and disinformation in competition.

2.1.4 Surprise: how the creation of surprise depends on the nature of information.

2.2 Information Gathering: gathering competitive information.

2.2.1 Personal Relationships: why information depends on personal relationships.

2.2.3 Standard Terminology: how mental models must be shared to enable communication.

2.3 Personal Interactions: making progress through personal interactions.

2.3.4 Using Questions: using questions in gathering information and predicting reactions.

2.3.5 Infinite Loops: predicting reactions on the basis of the "you-know-that-I-know-that-you-know" problem.

2.3.6 Promises and Threats: the use of promises and threats as strategic moves.

2.4 Contact Networks: the range of contacts needed to create perspective.

2.4.1 Ground Perspective: getting information on a new competitive arena.

2.4.2 Climate Perspective: getting perspective on temporary external conditions.

2.4.3 Command Perspective: developing sources for understanding decision-makers.

2.4.4 Methods Perspective: developing contacts who understand best practices.

2.4.5 Mission Perspective: how we develop and use a perspective on motivation.

2.5 The Big Picture: building big-picture strategic awareness.

2.6 Knowledge Leverage: getting competitive value out of knowledge.

2.7 Information Secrecy: defining the role of secrecy in relationships.

Glossary of Key Strategic Concepts

This glossary is keyed to the most common English words used in the translation of *The Art of War*. Those terms only capture the strategic concepts generally. Though translated as English nouns, verbs, adverbs, or adjectives, the Chinese characters on which they are based are totally conceptual, not parts of speech. For example, the character for CONFLICT is translated as the noun "conflict," as the verb "fight," and as the adjective "disputed." Ancient written Chinese was a conceptual language, not a spoken one. More like mathematical terms, these concepts are primarily defined by the strict structure of their relationships with other concepts. The Chinese names shown in parentheses with the characters are primarily based on Pinyin, but we occasionally use Cantonese terms to make each term unique.

ADVANCE (JEUN 進): to move into new GROUND; to expand your POSITION; to move forward in a campaign; the opposite of FLEE.

ADVANTAGE, *benefit* (LI 利): an opportunity arising from having a better POSITION relative to an ENEMY; an opening left by an ENEMY; a STRENGTH that matches against an ENEMY'S WEAKNESS; where fullness meets emptiness; a desirable characteristic of a strategic POSITION.

AIM, *vision, foresee* (JIAN 見): FOCUS on a specific ADVANTAGE, opening, or opportunity; predicting movements of an ENEMY; a skill of a LEADER in observing CLIMATE.

ANALYSIS, *plan* (GAI 計): a comparison of relative POSITION; the examination of the five factors that define a strategic POSITION; a combination of KNOWLEDGE and VISION; the ability to see through DECEPTION.

ARMY: see WAR.

ATTACK, *invade* (GONG 攻): a movement to new GROUND; advancing a strategic POSITION; action against an ENEMY in the sense of moving into his GROUND; opposite of DEFEND; does not necessarily mean CONFLICT.

BAD, *ruined* (PI 圮): a condition of the GROUND that makes ADVANCE difficult; destroyed; terrain that is broken and difficult to traverse; one of the nine situations or types of terrain.

BARRICADED: see OBSTACLES.

BATTLE (ZHAN 戰): to challenge; to engage an ENEMY; generically, to meet a challenge; to choose a confrontation with an ENEMY at a specific time and place; to focus all your resources on a task; to establish superiority in a POSITION; to challenge an ENEMY to increase CHAOS; that which is CONTROLLED by SURPRISE; one of the

four forms of ATTACK; the response to a DESPERATE SITUATION; character meaning was originally "big meeting," though later took on the meaning "big weapon"; not necessarily CONFLICT.

BRAVERY, *courage* (YONG 勇): the ability to face difficult choices; the character quality that deals with the changes of CLIMATE; courage of conviction; willingness to act on vision; one of the six characteristics of a leader.

BREAK, *broken, divided* (PO 破): to DIVIDE what is COMPLETE; the absence of a UNITING PHILOSOPHY; the opposite of UNITY.

CALCULATE, *count* (SHU 數): mathematical comparison of quantities and qualities; a measurement of DISTANCE or troop size.

CHANGE, *transform* (BIAN 變): transition from one CONDITION to another; the ability to adapt to different situations; a natural characteristic of CLIMATE.

CHAOS, *disorder* (JUAN 亂): CONDITIONS that cannot be FORESEEN; the natural state of confusion arising from BATTLE; one of six weaknesses of an organization; the opposite of CONTROL.

CLAIM, *position, form* (XING 形): to use the GROUND; a shape or specific condition of GROUND; the GROUND that you CONTROL; to use the benefits of the GROUND; the formations of troops; one of the four key skills in making progress.

CLIMATE, *heaven* (TIAN 天): the passage of time; the realm of uncontrollable CHANGE; divine providence; the weather; trends that CHANGE over time; generally, the future; what one must AIM at in the future; one of five key factors in ANALYSIS; the opposite of GROUND.

COMMAND (LING 令): to order or the act of ordering subordinates; the decisions of a LEADER; the creation of METHODS.

COMPETITION: see WAR.

COMPLETE: see UNITY.

CONDITION: see GROUND.

CONFINED, *surround* (WEI 圍): to encircle; a SITUATION or STAGE in which your options are limited; the proper tactic for dealing with an ENEMY that is ten times smaller; to seal off a smaller ENEMY; the characteristic of a STAGE in which a larger FORCE can be attacked by a smaller one; one of nine SITUATIONS or STAGES.

CONFLICT, *fight* (ZHENG 爭): to contend; to dispute; direct confrontation of arms with an ENEMY; highly desirable GROUND that creates disputes; one of nine types of GROUND, terrain, or stages.

CONSTRICTED, *narrow* (AI 狹): a confined space or niche; one of six field positions; the limited extreme of the dimension distance; the opposite of SPREAD-OUT.

CONTROL, *govern* (CHI 治): to manage situations; to overcome disorder; the opposite of CHAOS.

DANGEROUS: see SERIOUS.

DANGERS, *adverse* (AK 阨): a condition that makes it difficult to ADVANCE; one of three dimensions used to evaluate advantages; the dimension with the extreme field POSITIONS of ENTANGLING and SUPPORTING.

DEATH, *desperate* (SI 死): to end or the end of life or efforts; an extreme situation in which the only option is BATTLE; one of nine STAGES or types of TERRAIN; one of five types of SPIES; opposite of SURVIVE.

DECEPTION, *bluffing, illusion* (GUI 詭): to control perceptions; to control information; to mislead an ENEMY; an attack on an opponent's AIM; the characteristic of war that confuses perceptions.

DEFEND (SHOU 守): to guard or to hold a GROUND; to remain in a POSITION; the opposite of ATTACK.

DETOUR (YU 迂): the indirect or unsuspected path to a POSITION; the more difficult path to ADVANTAGE; the route that is not DIRECT.

DIRECT, *straight* (JIK 直): a straight or obvious path to a goal; opposite of DETOUR.

DISTANCE, *distant* (YUAN 遠): the space separating GROUND; to be remote from the current location; to occupy POSITIONS that are not close to one another; one of six field positions; one of the three dimensions for evaluating opportunities; the emptiness of space.

DIVIDE, *separate* (FEN 分): to break apart a larger force; to separate from a larger group; the opposite of JOIN and FOCUS.

DOUBLE AGENT, *reverse* (FAN 反): to turn around in direction; to change a situation; to switch a person's allegiance; one of five types of spies.

EASY, *light* (QING 輕): to require little effort; a SITUATION that requires little effort; one of nine STAGES or types of terrain; opposite of SERIOUS.

EMOTION, *feeling* (XIN 心): an unthinking reaction to AIM, a necessary element to inspire MOVES; a component of esprit de corps; never a sufficient cause for ATTACK.

ENEMY, *competitor* (DIK 敵): one who makes the same CLAIM; one with a similar GOAL; one with whom comparisons of capabilities are made.

ENTANGLING, *hanging* (GUA 懸): a POSITION that cannot be returned to; any CONDITION that leaves no easy place to go; one of six field positions.

EVADE, *avoid* (BI 避): the tactic used by small competitors when facing large opponents.

FALL APART, *collapse* (BENG 崩): to fail to execute good decisions; to fail to use a CONSTRICTED POSITION; one of six weaknesses of an organization.

FALL DOWN, *sink* (HAAM 陷): to fail to make good decisions; to MOVE from a SUPPORTING POSITION; one of six weaknesses of organizations.

FEELINGS, *affection, love* (CHING 情): the bonds of relationship; the result of a shared PHILOSOPHY; requires management.

FIGHT, *struggle* (DOU 鬥): to engage in CONFLICT; to face difficulties.

FIRE (HUO 火): an environmental weapon; a universal analogy for all weapons.

FLEE, *retreat, northward* (BEI 北): to abandon a POSITION; to surrender GROUND; one of six weaknesses of an ARMY; opposite of ADVANCE.

FOCUS, *concentrate* (ZHUAN 專): to bring resources together at a given time; to UNITE forces for a purpose; an attribute of having a shared PHILOSOPHY; the opposite of *divide*.

FORCE (LEI 力): power in the simplest sense; a GROUP of people bound by UNITY and FOCUS; the relative balance of STRENGTH in opposition to WEAKNESS.

FORESEE: see AIM.

FULLNESS: see STRENGTH.

GENERAL: see LEADER.

GOAL: see PHILOSOPHY.

GROUND, *situation, stage* (DI 地): the earth; a specific place; a specific condition; the place one competes; the prize of competition; one of five key factors in competitive analysis; the opposite of CLIMATE.

GROUPS, *troops* (DUI 隊): a number of people united under a shared PHILOSOPHY; human resources of an organization; one of the five targets of fire attacks.

INSIDE, *internal* (NEI 內): within a TERRITORY or organization; an insider; one of five types of spies; opposite of OUTSIDE.

INTERSECTING, *highway* (QU 衢): a SITUATION or GROUND that allows you to JOIN; one of nine types of terrain.

JOIN (HAP 合): to unite; to make allies; to create a larger FORCE; opposite of DIVIDE.

KNOWLEDGE, *listening* (ZHI 知): to have information; the result of listening; the first step in advancing a POSITION; the basis of strategy.

LAX, *loosen* (SHII 弛): too easygoing; lacking discipline; one of six weaknesses of an army.

LEADER, *general, commander* (JIANG 將): the decision-maker in a competitive unit; one who LISTENS and AIMS; one who manages TROOPS; superior of officers and men; one of the five key factors in analysis; the conceptual opposite of SYSTEM, the established methods, which do not require decisions.

LEARN, *compare* (XIAO 效): to evaluate the relative qualities of ENEMIES.

LISTEN, *obey* (TING 聽): to gather KNOWLEDGE; part of ANALYSIS.

LISTENING: see KNOWLEDGE.

LOCAL, *countryside* (XIANG 鄉): the nearby GROUND; to have KNOWLEDGE of a specific GROUND; one of five types of SPIES.

MARSH (ZE 澤): GROUND where footing is unstable; one of the four types of GROUND; analogy for uncertain situations.

METHOD: see SYSTEM.

MISSION: see PHILOSOPHY.

MOMENTUM, *influence* (SHI 勢): the FORCE created by SURPRISE set up by STANDARDS; used with TIMING.

MOUNTAINS, *hill, peak* (SHAN 山): uneven GROUND; one of four types of GROUND; an analogy for all unequal SITUATIONS.

MOVE, *march, act* (HANG 行): action toward a position or goal.

NATION (GUO 國): the state; the productive part of an organization; the seat of political power; the entity that controls an ARMY or competitive part of the organization.

OBSTACLES, *barricaded* (XIAN 險): to have barriers; one of the three characteristics of the GROUND; one of six field positions; as a field position, opposite of UNOBSTRUCTED.

OPEN, *meeting, crossing* (JIAO 來): to share the same GROUND without conflict; to come together; a SITUATION that encourages a race; one of nine TERRAINS or STAGES.

OPPORTUNITY: see ADVANTAGE.

OUTMANEUVER (SOU 走): to go astray; to be FORCED into a WEAK POSITION; one of six weaknesses of an army.

OUTSIDE, *external* (WAI 外): not within a TERRITORY or ARMY; one who has a different perspective; one who offers an objective view; opposite of INTERNAL.

PHILOSOPHY, *mission, goals* (TAO 道): the shared GOALS that UNITE an ARMY; a system of thought; a shared viewpoint; literally "the way"; a way to work together; one of the five key factors in ANALYSIS.

PLATEAU (LIU 陸): a type of GROUND without defects; an analogy for any equal, solid, and certain SITUATION; the best place for competition; one of the four types of GROUND.

RESOURCES, *provisions* (LIANG 糧): necessary supplies, most commonly food; one of the five targets of fire attacks.

RESTRAINT: see TIMING.

REWARD, *treasure, money* (BAO 賞): profit; wealth; the necessary compensation for competition; a necessary ingredient for

VICTORY; VICTORY must pay.

SCATTER, *dissipating* (SAN 散): to disperse; to lose UNITY; the pursuit of separate GOALS as opposed to a central MISSION; a situation that causes a FORCE to scatter; one of nine conditions or types of terrain.

SERIOUS, *heavy* (CHONG 重): any task requiring effort and skill; a SITUATION where resources are running low when you are deeply committed to a campaign or heavily invested in a project; a situation where opposition within an organization mounts; one of nine STAGES or types of TERRAIN.

SIEGE (GONG CHENG 攻城): to move against entrenched positions; any movement against an ENEMY'S STRENGTH; literally "strike city"; one of the four forms of attack; the least desirable form of attack.

SITUATION: see GROUND.

SPEED, *hurry* (SAI 馳): to MOVE over GROUND quickly; the ability to ADVANCE POSITIONS in a minimum of time; needed to take advantage of a window of opportunity.

SPREAD-OUT, *wide* (GUANG 廣): a surplus of DISTANCE; one of the six GROUND POSITIONS; opposite of CONSTRICTED.

SPY, *conduit, go-between* (GAAN 間): a source of information; a channel of communication; literally, an "opening between."

STAGE: see GROUND.

STANDARD, *proper, correct* (JANG 正): the expected behavior; the standard approach; proven methods; the opposite of SURPRISE; together with SURPRISE creates MOMENTUM.

STOREHOUSE, *house* (KU 庫): a place where resources are stockpiled; one of the five targets for fire attacks.

STORES, *accumulate, savings* (JI 糧): resources that have been stored; any type of inventory; one of the five targets of fire attacks.

STRENGTH, *fullness, satisfaction* (SAT 壹): wealth or abundance or resources; the state of being crowded; the opposite of XU, empty.

SUPPLY WAGONS, *transport* (ZI 輜): the movement of RESOURCES through DISTANCE; one of the five targets of fire attacks.

SUPPORT, *supporting* (ZHII 支): to prop up; to enhance; a GROUND POSITION that you cannot leave without losing STRENGTH; one of six field positions; the opposite extreme of ENTANGLING.

SURPRISE, *unusual, strange* (QI 奇): the unexpected; the innovative; the opposite of STANDARD; together with STANDARDS creates MOMENTUM.

SURROUND: see CONFINED.

SURVIVE, *live, birth* (SHAANG 生): the state of being created, started, or beginning; the state of living or surviving; a temporary condition of fullness; one of five types of spies; the opposite of DEATH.

SYSTEM, *method* (FA 法): a set of procedures; a group of techniques; steps to accomplish a GOAL; one of the five key factors in analysis; the realm of groups who must follow procedures; the opposite of the LEADER.

TERRITORY, *terrain*: see GROUND.

TIMING, *restraint* (JIE 節): to withhold action until the proper time; to release tension; a companion concept to MOMENTUM.

TROOPS: see GROUPS.

UNITY, *whole, oneness* (YI 一): the characteristic of a GROUP that shares a PHILOSOPHY; the lowest number; a GROUP that acts as a unit; the opposite of DIVIDED.

UNOBSTRUCTED, *expert* (TONG 通): without obstacles or barriers; GROUND that allows easy movement; open to new ideas; one of six field positions; opposite of OBSTRUCTED.

VICTORY, *win, winning* (SING 勝): success in an endeavor; getting a reward; serving your mission; an event that produces more than it consumes; to make a profit.

WAR, *competition, army* (BING 兵): a dynamic situation in which POSITIONS can be won or lost; a contest in which a REWARD can be won; the conditions under which the rules of strategy work.

WATER, *river* (SHUI 水): a fast-changing GROUND; fluid CONDITIONS; one of four types of GROUND; an analogy for change.

WEAKNESS, *emptiness, need* (XU 虛): the absence of people or resources; devoid of FORCE; the point of ATTACK for an ADVANTAGE; a characteristic of GROUND that enables SPEED; poor; the opposite of STRENGTH.

WIN, *winning*: see VICTORY.

WIND, *fashion, custom* (FENG 風): the pressure of environmental forces.

Index of Topics in *The Art of War*

This index identifies significant topics, keyed to the chapters, block numbers (big numbers in text), and line numbers (tiny numbers). The format is chapter:block.lines.

About the Author

Gary Gagliardi

This book's award-winning translator and primary author, Gary Gagliardi, is America's leading authority on Sun Tzu's *The Art of War*. A frequent guest on radio and television talk shows, Gary has written over wenty books on strategy. Ten of his books on Sun Tzu's methods have won award recognition in business, self-help, career, sports, philosophy, multicultural, and youth nonfiction categories.

Gary began studying Sun Tzu's philosophy over thirty years ago. His understanding of strategy was proven in the business world, where his software company became one of the Inc. 500 fastest-growing companies in America and won numerous business awards. After selling his software company, Gary began writing about and teaching Sun Tzu's strategic philosophy full time.

He has spoken all over the world on a variety of topics concerning competition, from modern technology to ancient history. His books have been translated into many languages, including Japanese, Thai, Korean, Russian, Indonesian, and Spanish.

Today he splits his time between Seattle and Las Vegas, living with his wife, Rebecca, and travels extensively for speaking engagements all over the world.

garyg@suntzus.com

@strategygary

Want to learn more about Sun Tzu's strategy?

SunTzuS.com

SCIENCE OF STRATEGY INSTITUTE

eBooks

Audio books

Audio seminars

Online training

Art of War and Strategy Books By Gary Gagliardi

Sun Tzu's Art of War Rule Book in Nine Volumes

Sun Tzu's The Art of War Plus The Art of Sales: Strategy for the Sales Warrior

9 Formulas for Business Success: the Science of Strategy

The Golden Key to Strategy: Everyday Strategy for Everyone

The Art of War Plus The Chinese Revealed

The Art of War Plus The Art of Management: Straegy for Management Warriors

Art of War for Warrior Marketing: Strategy for Conquering Markets

The Art of War Plus The Art of Politics: Strategy for Campaigns (with Shawn Frost)

Making Money By Speaking: The Spokesperson Strategy

The Warrior Class: 306 Lessons in Strategy

The Art of War for the Business Warrior: Strategy for Entrepreneurs

The Art of War Plus The Warrior's Apprentice: Strategy for Teens

The Art of War Plus Strategy for Sales Managers: Strategy for Sales Groups

The Ancient Bing-fa: Martial Arts Strategy

Strategy Against Terror: Ancient Wisdom for Today's War

The Art of War Plus The Art of Career Building: Strategy for Promotion

Sun Tzu's Art of War Plus Parenting Teens

The Art of War Plus Its Amazing Secrets: The Keys to Ancient Chinese Science

Art of War Plus Art of Love: Strategy for Romance

www.ingramcontent.com/pod-product-compliance
Lightning Source LLC
Chambersburg PA
CBHW070509200326
41519CB00013B/2764